THE NATION AND THE KINGDOM

Charles W. Forman

The NATION and

To MY MOTHER

the KINGDOM

Christian Mission in the New Nations

FRIENDSHIP PRESS

New York

it means for us. The nations at that time were the major groupings of mankind possessing a common language, culture, and religion. They were not usually political units as they are today. The political units were either smaller, such as the city-states within the Greek nation, or much larger, like the Roman Empire, which encompassed many nations. Not till centuries later in Western Europe did the nation and the state coalesce into the nation-state, which we know today. But in biblical times, as now, the nations did represent the principal divisions of mankind. Therefore, the Bible's way of looking at those groupings has implications for the way in which we look at our great divisions.

At the beginning of the Bible's story the division of men into nations is presented as both a natural part of God's created order, arising out of the many families of mankind (Genesis 10) and also as a punishment for human pride and self-sufficiency (Genesis 11). At the end of the story the nations are pictured as bringing their glory and honor into the city of God (Revelation 21:24-26). The books in between never forget the fact that men live as members of nations. They refer to mankind beyond Israel as "the nations" rather than with words suggesting an undifferentiated mass. When toward the end the Church was thrust into the human scene, it was viewed as a new people of God or even a new nation (I Peter 2:9) drawn from all the nations and overcoming all the separations between them (Galatians 3:28). It was given the task of making disciples of the nations (Matthew 28:19).

All this suggests a dual attitude toward the nations of which we are a part. The nations do have a place in God's

CONTENTS

Introduction: *NATION OR KINGDOM?*

THE country was Uganda. The year, 1962. Independence had just been proclaimed. In the mail for the bishop one day came a postcard from an unknown member of his church. Its simple words expressed the feelings which all Christians of the country shared at a time like that. It read:

May the Independence which we gained on 9th October bring you much blessing spiritually and physically and may it help you to do God's work well and to teach people to love Him above all things and our neighbors as ourselves.[1]

These words strike a response in the hearts of all of us, whatever our nation may be. It is our hope, too, that the life of our nation may prove a blessing to all our people and to all our neighbors.

But how is this to be?

[1] Quoted in S. W. Baron, *Modern Nationalism and Religion*, p. 140. New York: Harper and Brothers, 1947.

As Christians we have been told to "seek first the Kingdom of God." We wonder what place our nation has in that Kingdom. How can we love and serve our nation and at the same time love and serve the wider Kingdom which includes all mankind? Perhaps the nation and that Kingdom fit easily and naturally together. If they do, then it will be easy to serve them jointly. Obedience to God will include the fostering of a strong loyalty to our nation and to its purposes and spirit. This seems to be the implication of a statement by the famous theologian, Friederich Schleiermacher, who said, "Only that people relies on the Lord who wishes at all costs to preserve the peculiar purpose and spirit with which He has endowed it."

But perhaps the two do not fit together so naturally. "No man can serve two masters." Does the nation present itself to us as an alternative master? Must we choose between it and the Kingdom? Obedience to God's Kingdom does in fact make us look beyond our nation with its peculiar purpose and spirit to the wider concerns of all men. This is the emphasis of Karl Barth's statement: "The Church will be the last to lend its support to mere parochial politics. . . . In the Church we have tasted the air of freedom and must bring others to taste it, too." [2] Can this wider concern be harmonized with full loyalty to the nation? Or must we discount the nation in order to live by the higher loyalty? Here is a region of our perplexity.

When we look to the Bible for light on the place of the nation, we encounter difficulties. The word "nation" did not mean quite the same thing in the ancient world that

---

[2] Barth, Karl. *Community, State, and the Church*, p. 178. New York: Doubleday and Co., Inc., 1960.

purpose for us even though they are in some respects a necessary handicap, which we must suffer. Their existence is to be recognized in the preaching of the gospel, though they are never to stand in the way of fellowship between Christians. We are not to ignore them or the development of their peculiar purposes and spirit, but we are to remember that their honor is eventually to be brought into God's Kingdom. The purposes of the nations are to be judged by the standards of that Kingdom.

The final judgment is made by God himself. But tentative judgments must also be made from day to day by Christians living in their various nations. For the most part these judgments in recent years have had to be negative. The infection of mass hysteria, the flames of bombed cities, and the gas chambers of extermination programs have marked the recent course of nationalism in the Western world. For many Christians coming out of such an experience, the purposes of the nations are revealed in such a negative light that they find it nearly impossible to make any positive judgment even on the existence of nations.

But side by side with this disenchantment in the West a very different kind of experience with the nation has been filling the lives of Christians in Asia and Africa. Though they have met many difficulties in national life, they have also found for themselves a deep sense of liberation, a widened sense of community, and a fuller range of service to men as national feeling has grown among them. They, therefore, make a much more positive judgment on the nation. For them it is more natural to see the place of the nation in the purpose of God. Doubtless they will need to be saved from future disillusionment by learning more of the tragic course of nationalism in the Western world. But they have something to teach as well as something to learn. They can show us the other side of the dual attitude, which has been lost by many thoughtful Christians in the West. They can do much to redeem for us our life in the nation and the whole sense of nationality.

The flash of their feelings is shown in the declaration of the All-Africa Christian Youth Assembly of 1963:

We rejoice in the pursuit by the peoples of Africa of freedom: freedom from the bondage of ignorance, poverty, oppression and disease. We share as Christians the destiny of Africa, and the responsibility to help in developing our nations. Standing side by side in solidarity with our fellow men, and sharing our common human aspirations for better social and economic life, we will point out to them and to ourselves the true freedom that God, in Christ, has offered to mankind. We affirm that all human quests for freedom are judged and fulfilled in the freedom of him who died on the Cross and rose from the dead. It is his service that is perfect freedom. We will declare with our lips and show forth through our lives the Gospel of the good news of freedom for Africa.[3]

If we would truly love our nation and faithfully seek the Kingdom of God, it behooves us to pay attention to the experience of Christians in the new nations.

[3] "Message of the All-Africa Christian Youth Assembly," *Ecumenical Review*, Vol. XV, No. 3, p. 332.

1

CHRISTIANITY AND THE FOUNDATIONS FOR NEW NATIONS

THE achievement of independence by any nation has always been regarded as a landmark in the course of human history. In our rapidly moving times landmarks of this kind, like all others, are passed with unbelievable rapidity. "Independence days" have come as frequently as eighteen in a single year. That number, which is surely an all-time record, since it can scarcely be equaled in the future, was reached in the year 1960. But quite aside from that year, with its dramatic roster of political turnovers, the whole period since the Second World War has been marked by the emergence of new nations in unprecedented numbers.

Immediately upon the close of the war Syria and Lebanon appeared as independent nations, the reduced French forces being unable to reassert their former domination in that region. Korea emerged from under Japanese control at the same time. Then, in 1946, the British suzerainty over Jordan was withdrawn, and the United States fulfilled an earlier commitment by giving independence to the Philippines. These developments indicated the direction that events would take. The great change began with the transfer of power in India in 1947. India was "the brightest jewel in the British crown," by far the largest and most valuable dependency in all the empires of the world. The Indian people had been in advance of all the colonial peoples in the struggle against European rule. Therefore, when the British government, recognizing the problems of continued domination and seeking a more hopeful relationship, decided to grant freedom to India, it was as if the keystone in the arch of imperialism had been withdrawn. Forces were released and claims were legitimized that meant that the remainder of the structure was bound to come down. Both Asia and Africa were newly aroused.

The freedom of India, of course, included the freedom of Pakistan, which had formed part of the same governmental unit prior to independence. The decision on India involved also an identical decision for Ceylon and Burma, the latter of which had been administered as part of India during most of the British rule. Actual independence came for both Ceylon and Burma in 1948. Palestine, which had been a bone of contention between Arab and Jew, followed in 1949, being freed and divided simultaneously, like India. The same year saw the final withdrawal of the Dutch from Indonesia after four years of warfare and confusion. Similarly, in Indo-China years of bitter fighting preceded the departure of the French forces in 1954 when the independence of Viet Nam, Cambodia, and Laos was recognized. The last of Asia's nations to become independent was Malaya.[1] The structures for its self-government had been established in 1948 when all of the Malay states were brought into a single federation, but the consummation of full independence did not come till 1957. That year marked the end of colonial control over the countries of Asia. It must be added, however, that there were parts of two islands, Borneo and New Guinea, which were not absorbed by the independent countries until later and that there were still in that year five Asian cities which remained under European control: Aden, Goa, Singapore, Macao, and Hong Kong.

The year the decolonization process concluded in Asia was also the year of its beginning in tropical Africa. Ghana, the first of the nations of tropical Africa to break away from European rule, became independent in 1957. At the time of independence the Prime Minister of Ghana was at pains to point out that this event was but the prelude to general independence for all the colonial territories of Africa and that he regarded the freedom of Ghana as meaningless apart from the freedom of the whole continent. His expectations were rapidly fulfilled. The Sudan and the North African states of Libya, Tunisia, and Morocco, which are culturally more a part of the Middle East, had already broken from foreign control, and the break in Ghana started a precipitous departure of colonialism from Africa south of the Sahara. In 1958 Guinea became the first country to break away from the French area of tropical Africa.

[1] In 1963, Malaya became a part of the newly formed Federation of Malaysia.

Then came 1960, the record year, with

Cameroun
Central African Republic
Chad
Congo (Leopoldville)
Congo (Brazzaville)
Dahomey
Gabon
Ivory Coast
Malagasy Republic
Mali
Mauritania
Niger
Nigeria
Senegal
Somaliland
Togo
Upper Volta

Outside Africa, Cyprus became independent in 1960, too.

This spate of new nations naturally resulted in a slowing down of the process in the next years. The 1961 crop of new African nations numbered only two—Sierra Leone and Tanganyika. The year 1962 saw four more African states emerge, Uganda, Rwanda, and Burundi, a group of neighbors in the east, and Algeria in the north. Also in 1962 the independence of Western Samoa marked the first break from empire in the Pacific islands. Two island republics in the West Indies, Jamaica and Trinidad-Tobago, also joined the list, leaving relatively few countries still scheduled to become independent.

THE BIRTH OF NATIONAL FEELING

The hour of independence is, of course, only the culmination of a long process by which a new nation comes into existence. No one can understand the achievement of independence in a new nation by looking at that achievement alone. The foundation on which it is built must be examined, the long years during which the sense of being a nation and of having a right to independence are developed among the people. In Europe and the areas of European settlement those years stretched over centuries. In other parts of the world the foundations of national feeling were laid much later but developed much faster. Until fairly recently the people in what are now the new nations continued to live for the most part in the traditional relationships, the ancient type of "nation," which was also prevalent in Europe before the rise of nation-states. They thought of themselves in terms of religious communities, tribal communities, families, castes, or the like, and were not strongly conscious of being nations in political-territorial units. As late as 1952 the principal political figure of Western Nigeria, Chief Awolowo, said of his country, "Nigeria is not a nation. It is a mere political expression."

This was very late for such a statement to be made, but a half century earlier the same remark could have been made about most of the areas that now constitute the new nations of the world. To be sure, there had been revolts against the European control, but these were not really national revolts. The so-called Indian Mutiny of 1857 or the Boxer Rebellion in China in 1900, the Saya San rebellion of 1931 in Burma, or the terrorizing "fahavalo" of

1896 in Madagascar all showed the hatred of the people for European rule. But these were rebellions led by and carried out in the name of the old order. The Rani of Jhansi in India, the secret society in China, the Buddhist monks in Burma, the medicine men and tribal chiefs in Africa and Madagascar all were symbols of an old order that resisted the encroachments of the modern world and rebelled against it. They were not national movements in the strict sense of the term because the nation had not yet become conscious of itself. But these rebellions all failed. It was not till the modern idea of the nation appeared on the scene that a force was created powerful enough to eject the foreign rulers.

National sentiment developed at different times in different areas. It grew powerful in India before it had strength in Burma or Indonesia. It was widespread throughout Asia before it had even appeared in Africa. The First World War with its emphasis on the freedom of peoples and self-determination for European nations provided the stimulus for the greatest surge of nationalism in Asia. The Second World War played the same role in the case of Africa.

A striking thing about the idea of the nation is that though it was directed against European rule it was very largely imported from Europe. The national revolutions could not be regarded as struggles for the old order because they were themselves expressions of the new. So the ejection of Europe in a sense marked the triumph of Europe. The leaders of the movement for independence have all been men of Western education, and all, except Gandhi, have frankly advocated the patterning of their national life on Western models. Even the exception of Gandhi has not proved significant, since those who finally achieved power on the basis of his labors discarded his plans for a return to the past and set their faces firmly in the direction of the modern nation-state.

These leaders actually received their sense of nationalism through Western education. In their textbooks they were introduced to ideals of human freedom and equality, and they began to hold up these ideals for themselves and their compatriots. After receiving such inspiration, they then had the bitter experience of running into many denials of these ideals by the very rulers who taught them. A highly educated and cultured gentleman upon entering a railway carriage might find his way blocked by a boorish European who denied him entrance simply because of his color and nationality. Out of this combination of high ideals and hard experience the flames of national feeling began to arise. The most complete study that has been made of the development of national consciousness in the new nations, Rupert Emerson's *From Empire to Nation,* confirms the belief that it was these ideals and experiences rather than any economic needs or other factors that were the real wellspring of the national revolution in Asia and Africa.

DEEP ROOTS

If it is true that the national spirit grew out of certain beliefs about man, it inevitably grew up with a certain relationship to the Christian belief about man. The national movement has had its relationships to other religions, of course. National leaders have often used the traditional religion of their country as a rallying point for their activities. So the first national movement in Indonesia bore the name of a religious body, the Sarekat Islam, and Sukarno first came to fame through his efforts to carry out a nationwide campaign for the building of a great mosque as a national symbol. In Africa the famous nationalist leader, Jomo Kenyatta, dedicated his principal book "for perpetuation of communion with ancestral spirits . . . and in the firm faith that the dead, the living, and the unborn will unite to rebuild the destroyed shrines." Christianity could hardly be related to national feeling in that way because it was not the traditional faith in the emerging nations. It was usually the traditional faith of the imperial powers. Yet, though Christianity was so separated from emerging nationhood at the superficial level, at the deeper level of its beliefs and teachings, it had very close relationships to the national spirit—so much so that the rise of that spirit cannot be adequately explained apart from direct or indirect reference to Christianity.

The very fact that it was ideas about human equality and human freedom that underlay the national movement suggests a relationship to the Christian teaching that men are equal before God and are free in Christ. As these ideas have appeared in the new nations, they have a more direct relationship, it must be admitted, to great social events like the French and American Revolutions and to the writings of men like Edmund Burke and John Stuart Mill. But the religious tie cannot be ignored.

The idea of human equality clearly has roots in the belief that "God shows no partiality" (Acts 10:34-35). This conviction does not mean that men are to be regarded as equal in strength or ability or intelligence but only that they are equally entitled to consideration. At first sight this belief seems to be concerned purely with individual equality and to be unrelated to national independence. But, as Barbara Ward has pointed out in her recent book, *The Rich Nations and the Poor Nations,* belief in the equality of individuals is easily extended to belief in the equality of groups of individuals, *i.e.,* nations. The national revolution actually became a form of expression of the doctrine of human equality. Men who had been taught that all human beings should be given equal consideration found that there were certain groups of human beings who were disregarded or disdained because they did not belong to the ruling nation. A national revolution was their reply. Of course, instances of disregard and disdain by the rulers for the ruled were nothing new in any of these societies. The new thing was the teaching about human equality, which had deep roots in the Christian faith.

The freedom of the Christian man also stimulated a belief in freedom and independence for the nation. This was not just by way of the analogy of one freedom with another. The connection went deeper than that. In Christ God has treated man as a free being, coming to him not in overpowering might but in love and leaving with him the responsibility as a free person to respond or not to respond. Whoever meets God in Christ then knows himself to be a free person because he has been confronted with the responsibility for a decision. He must treat other people also as if they were responsible, for he knows that they, too, are addressed by God in Christ. Out of this comes a demand for national freedom. If men are going to act responsibly in the world and treat others as if they were responsible, then they must be in a position to manage their own affairs both individually and as a group. The determination of affairs by a foreign power reduces their range of responsibility. Therefore, responsible citizens and a responsible society call for independence, and in this way the Christian belief in freedom leads to support for national freedom.

TIME WILL TELL

Another element of Christian belief that has served as a foundation for the development of national consciousness has been the Christian attitude toward human history. Both the Christian way of looking backward and the way of looking forward on the stream of human events has had an effect favorable to the sense of nationality. First consider the Christian attitude toward the past. Christianity has often been called an historical religion, meaning that it is grounded in certain historical events, such as the coming of Christ. It must therefore regard history as tremendously important. God's own concern for the affairs of human history as evidenced in the incarnation is reason enough to give the Christian a concern for human history. In areas of the world where the predominant religion has regarded the visible world as unimportant and human history as an endless and pointless cycle, as Hinduism and Buddhism have traditionally done, this Christian concern for history has helped to provide a radically new outlook. History, which might previously have been a largely neglected subject, has become something worthy of the most diligent study and profound consideration. This has had its serious effects in the development of national consciousness. The people who had had little knowledge of their past and little realization of what they had been became filled with a new sense of themselves through a knowledge of their history. Only when the national history had been dug up could a people begin to respect themselves as a nation and think of themselves in national terms.

An example can be found in the way in which the people of Ghana came to a pride in their past and a sense of a significant national history. A British Methodist, a former missionary and principal of a mission school, wrote a book in 1926 in which he made the suggestion for the first time that the people of the southern part of the Gold Coast might be the descendants of the people of the old empire of Ghana that existed a thousand miles to the northwest many centuries ago. Rev. W. T. Balmer, who made this suggestion, based it on linguistic analysis and on tribal legends that spoke of a migration from such a distant center. The idea was widely accepted among the people and when the country became independent, it took the name of Ghana, thus expressing a sense of continuity with the past and of the importance of history for the life of the nation. The other people of West Africa to develop an early interest in their history were the Yorubas, the dominant people of Western Nigeria. In their case, too, it was a churchman, an African Anglican bishop, who first developed a theory about their origin suggesting that they originally came from Egypt.

And then there is the Christian attitude toward the future. The Christian teaching that the course of human events is moving toward a grand culmination that will reveal the final triumph of righteousness is of basic significance for national life. As long as men felt history led nowhere or simply revolved in a circle there was little incentive to work for change. But then came the belief that the course of human events is like a drama leading to a great and revealing conclusion in which truth finally shines through. With that the groundwork was laid for a drive to put an end to the injustices suffered through racial or national prejudices. Such effort would no longer be conceived as a futile stirring up of matters, which would eventually settle back into their old condition, but rather as a pointer to the final triumph of truth and justice. In this way the efforts to improve the condition of the nation and its people were given a basic sanction and encouragement.

A Burman leader once told Walter Freytag, chairman of the German Missions Council, that the great drive of national life in his country was "the hunger for justice." Dr. Freytag's response was that this remark revealed the new forward looking sense, which has permeated the old society and broken it up. There is a goal out ahead that judges the present way of life and pulls at it. The old society ordered human relations according to the way things had always been. The justification of a custom lay in its long practice. But now the justification must lie in something seen in the future rather than something seen in the past. The new attitude toward the future is no less crucial for nationhood than is the new attitude toward the past.

It should be clear from all this that the germinal ideas of Christianity had an effect in Asia and Africa far beyond the limited circle of those who became Christians. These ideas were conveyed through every contact with the West. They had their influence, though often in a much diluted or distorted form, on people who had never been touched by the church. Such people began to make demands that implied that all men were ultimately equal. They began to raise questions as to the direction in which history was moving, or more important, ought to move, which assumed that history had a goal. These demands and questions resulted in the permeation of the whole Western-educated segment of society with an outlook derived, at least distantly, from Christian beliefs. It was in this way that national feeling in its deepest roots was fed by basic concepts of the Christian faith.

"ACTIONS SPEAK LOUDER . . ."

Nor was it only the teachings of the Christian religion that helped to produce the national awakening. Some of the activities of the church as well contributed to this effect. The studies carried out by early missionaries of indigenous life and culture made people more conscious of their national identity. The missionaries achieved this effect particularly through the study of languages. When William Carey went to Bengal in 1793, he studied and developed the use of the Bengali language so that he became recognized as one of the founders of Bengali prose. The self-conscious development of the language doubtless had something to do with the fact that it was among the Bengalis that Indian nationalism first erupted.

Many are the African languages that have first been written down by Christian missionaries. The Twi language, which is used by most of the people of southern and central Ghana, was given its chief impetus as a written form of expression by the Basel missionaries. The church they founded has continued to identify itself to a large extent with that language so that when the government of the country wished to establish a bureau of African languages it was to one of the seminary-trained leaders of that church, C. A. Akrofi, that they turned for guidance. Other cultural expressions have also received attention. The Roman Catholic priest, Placide Tempels, has been one of the main spokesmen for Bantu culture and the most famous writer on Bantu philosophy. An African priest, Alexis Kagame, has followed Tempels' lead, doing in a more complete way for the culture of Rwanda what Tempels has attempted on a wider scale. Kagame has written numerous works on the history, poetry, philosophy, and politics of his country. A recent survey of African writing points out that all modern African literature begins with Christian belief, though it eventually turns away from it, disillusioned because of the injustices of the white man.[1]

Among the Arab nations American missionaries had an important role in the revival of Arabic literature and the classical Arabic language in the nineteenth century. Then local Christians in centers like Beirut and Cairo carried further the use of Arabic as a vehicle of modern expression and established publishing houses and newspapers of importance. Through these they spread abroad the feeling among Arabs of being a distinct people with a nationality based on language and culture. The Christians felt none of the religious tie to the Turkish rule or to the Turkish caliphate that was felt by their Muslim compatriots, and hence they were peculiarly well situated for developing Arab national feeling. They also had more contact with the West and imbibed its national outlook. Thus they were among the pioneers of the Arab national movement, which led later

[1] Jahn, Janheinz. *Muntu: An Outline of the New African Culture*, pp. 197-198. New York: Grove Press, 1961.

to the revolts that broke up the Turkish Empire and later still to the revolts against Western rule.

Many other activities of the church contributed in varying fashion to the development of national feeling. A number of the national songs or national anthems of the new nations, such as those of the Cameroun, Ghana, and Korea, have been written by people who were Christians, usually students in mission schools. The widespread program of social service carried on by the mission schools served to awaken students to the needs of the nation and thus to give them a deeper national concern. Experience in church government served as training for some political leaders, particularly in Africa.

Beyond the detailed patterns of church activity, the whole effort of missions for building up self-governing churches provided a faint foreshadowing of national self-government. As early as the middle of the nineteenth century leading missionary statesmen like Henry Venn and Rufus Anderson were announcing that missions must work toward the creation of free and self-governing churches. Such thoughts had scarcely entered the minds of the leading imperial statesmen at that time. Cardinal Lavigerie, the greatest inaugurator of Roman Catholic missions to Africa, said from the beginning of his work that the day would come when Africans would want to be their own rulers and Christian missions should contribute to that end.

It is clear, then, that Christianity was deeply related, both in its doctrine and in many of its practices, to the foundations of modern national life in Asia and Africa. This, of course, does not mean that Christians in those countries believed in or approved of the national movement when it appeared. They may have been quite unconscious of the more profound connections that they had with that movement. What they thought about it cannot be determined by investigating the implications of their doctrine or their work but only by examining what their attitudes toward nationhood actually were.

2

CHRISTIAN ATTITUDES
TOWARD NATIONHOOD

AT FIRST glance the church in the new nations would seem to be a most unpromising place to look for any positive evaluation of nationhood. If Christians of the West have tended in recent years toward negative judgments on the existence of nations, the Christians of Asia and Africa could hardly be expected, on the face of things, to provide any balance or corrective to those views. All the most obvious things in their situation seemed to conspire against any appreciation for the sense of nationhood as it emerged in their homelands.

Despite the deep connections that we have traced between Christian doctrines and national existence, we must recognize that the Christianity that came to Asia and Africa was of a type inclined to ignore nationality as a factor in human affairs. There are such things as Christian individualism and Christian universalism, and both of these had left their stamp upon that Christianity. These two emphases stand on either side of Christian concern for the nation. One stresses the importance of the individual, the other the importance of the whole world of men. Between them they can well produce a total blindness to the groupings in which men live. Individualism was dominant in the revivals that inspired the modern missionary movement, and universalism, in the sense of a concern for all mankind, was of the essence of that movement. With such powerful countervailing emphases present, there seemed to be little room for interest in the nation as an entity having legitimate aspirations of its own.

Then there were the circumstantial ties to imperialism, which militated against any acceptance of the new national spirit. An old tradition in European empires linked the church and the imperial power in close alliance. The Portuguese, Spanish, and Dutch empires of the sixteenth and seventeenth centuries all held to this tradition, and its influence could still be felt in some places in the twentieth century. The closest tie between imperial rule and Protestantism in the twentieth century, for example, was to be found in Indonesia where many of the old traditions of Dutch rule still prevailed. An official church, the Protestant Church of the Netherlands Indies, was maintained by the government. Its ministers habitually referred to their parish appointments in the same terms that civil servants referred to administrative appointments. In India, likewise, the Anglican Church received grants from the government, though these were almost entirely for the manning and maintenance of chaplaincies, similar to army chaplaincies, in the railway centers and cantonments where Englishmen traditionally resided. They were not meant for the provision of ministers and buildings for congregations of the indigenous inhabitants, such as the Dutch provided.

Educational and medical work developed under the imperial governments also made for close ties with Christian missions. In the early days these ties were minimal because empires were not interested in improving the capacities of their subjects. Missions looked to imperial powers only for the protection that stable government could provide. Even this much of a tie led missionaries in a number of cases to advocate imperial expansion. Then came the time of more active cooperation. In the very days when national sentiment was first appearing in the colonies, the "white man's burden" philosophy of empire began to spread among the European powers. The imperial rulers felt constrained to provide more public funds for welfare purposes and the missions that were carrying on welfare work received more government grants for their activities. It seemed natural when the empire was converted to an "ethical policy," as it was called in the Netherlands in the early years of this century, to look upon the imperial purpose and the missionary purpose as intertwined. Missions, it was suggested, should cooperate with empires as the best way available for serving the welfare of the people.

The contributions that missions rendered in fulfillment of the white man's burden were stressed in missionary writings. One of the major missionary societies of the Anglican Church, the Society for the Propagation of the Gospel, published in 1918 a group of missionary appeals with such telltale titles as *The Call of Empire* and *Imperial Christianity*, in which the example of political imperialism as an expression of the conviction of superiority was urged upon the church. All who were "alive to England's imperial task and to England's honor" were urged to support missions, though with the highly important qualification that this was to be done for the purpose of enabling the peoples of the Empires to participate more effectively in their own self-government.

Then, of course, there was the most obvious fact that the missionaries were themselves Europeans or people of European ancestry, like the imperial rulers. Most often they came from the very country that was the imperial overlord. This fact inclined the churches toward friendly relations with the imperial power and toward suspicion of nationalists. Occasionally the imperial connections of the missionary were played up very consciously. Hans-Werner Gensichen has shown how this was done when the Evangelical Missionary Society for German East Africa was founded in 1886 soon after Germany's entry into Africa. The appeals that were issued by the founders of the society called for "German work" serving "Church and Fatherland" carrying on "mission in a national German sense." [1] As long as Belgium ruled in Africa, the Roman Catholic missions in its territory were referred to as "national" missions while others were "foreign." Portugal required all missionaries who were not themselves Portuguese to spend a year of study in the European homeland before proceeding to the colonies.

EARLY ATTITUDES

Considering the weight of all these circumstances predisposing Christians against the national cause, the actual attitude adopted by missions and churches toward the sense

---

[1] Gensichen, Hans-Werner. "Die Deutsche Mission und der Kolonialismus," *Kerygma und Dogma*, Vol. 8 (1962), pp. 136-149.

of nationality when it first emerged is a considerable surprise. Their utterances were usually characterized by a genial appreciation for the national spirit. This was due in part to counterbalancing circumstances. Missionaries who worked for many years in a country gradually identified themselves with the viewpoint of their adopted land. R. Pierce Beaver, in a special study of this subject [2] has shown how missionaries normally became devoted to the land of their work and stood for its point of view even over that of their homeland. He has also shown how they emphasized the values of nationhood in the land where they worked.

The appreciation was due also to conviction. Christian belief in equality and freedom could not but have its effect. Gustav Warneck, who thought deeply on these matters and was the most respected German scholar of missions, opposed having any emphasis placed on "German work" and declared that no hint of imperial purposes should ever infect the missionary enterprise. The World Missionary Conference in Edinburgh in 1910 expressed Christian convictions based on the claims of Christ's principles, in favor of the national spirit when it said:

This national and racial spirit cannot and should not be crushed or checked. It is a matter of profound concern to the Christian Church. It will have much power to hinder or to facilitate the spread of Christ's Kingdom. Christ never by teaching or example resisted or withstood the spirit of true nationalism. Wherever His principles, including those pertaining to the supreme claims of His Kingdom on earth, have

[2] Beaver, R. Pierce, "Nationalism and Missions," *Church History*, Vol. 26 (1957), pp. 22-42.

had largest right of way, they have served to strengthen national spirit and not to weaken it.[3]

Such things were being said when national feeling was still in its infancy in Asia and Africa. How much more could they be expected to be proclaimed when the national movement was fully grown and was the center of everyone's attention. In the 1920's and 1930's the Christian support for national movements in the colonial lands increased. But the question became more complicated in those days because of the tragic experience with nationalism in Europe and in Japan. The horrors of the First World War followed by the excesses of fascism and nazism showed what dangers lurked in the seemingly innocent nationalism of 1910. Therefore the churches and missions became more discriminating in their attitude, approving the internationally minded and unmilitary national spirit that was found in the colonial lands but warning against the corruptions of the same sentiment in any land where nationalism became the religion.

The Oxford Conference of 1937 marked the high point of recent international Christian thought about the nation. It provided a clear expression of the more discriminating attitude that Christians were adopting. On the one hand it acknowledged the place of the nation as being one of the structures of human life ordained by God, and thereby it recognized by implication the legitimacy of Christian participation in the building up of a sense of nationhood among the colonial peoples. It said that, as a rule, the primary call

[3] World Missionary Conference, Edinburgh, 1910. *Report of Commission I, Carrying the Gospel to the Non-Christian World,* p. 33. Published for World Missionary Conference by Oliphant, Anderson and Ferrier.

on the loyalty of the individual Christian and of the church is from the community in which God has set them. But, on the other hand, the main burden of the conference report was in condemnation of militant and aggressive nationalism. Every form of national life that leads to the suppression of other nationalities (*i.e.,* imperialism) or to a failure to respect those nationalities was denounced as rebellion against God. Any attempt to make the nation the source of salvation was categorized as sin. The effort to bring unity and purpose into life by making the nation the center of all unity and purpose was attacked. Nationalism, it was stated, too often attempts to make the nation into God.

Such a report could give aid and encouragement to the growing sense of national identity among the colonial peoples while its criticism fell on the imperialistic and militant nationalism appearing in Europe. The great international missionary conferences held at Jerusalem and Madras in 1928 and 1938 took a position basically the same as that of Oxford. Little wonder that the devotees of absolutist nationalism, such as the Nazis, saw in Christian missions an ally of the national revolt against European imperialism. A Nazi journal declared, "Christianity with its theory of equality and redemption is a hindrance to the sovereignty of the white man. The greatest danger of the dethroning of white men and their political power comes from the teaching of missions." [4]

The Oxford Conference's views on Asian nationhood received fuller expression from one of the secretaries of the conference, William Paton, when he visited the East a short

---

[4] Editorial in *Schwarze Korps,* quoted in S. W. Baron, *Modern Nationalism and Religion,* p. 155. New York: Harper and Brothers, 1947.

time later. He was traveling as secretary of the International Missionary Council. In a report on his journey, entitled *Christianity in the Eastern Conflicts,* he had nothing but appreciative words for the national movements, though he recognized that the church must always be free to criticize any social movement. He maintained that, since God has made the community within which the church is set, the church should never try to lead a life apart from the community, and since the sense of nationality is the expression of the spirit of the community, the church should be in sympathy with it. The national feeling of a country like India, he said, was not to be confused with the aggressive nationalism seen elsewhere.

The situation in which foreign missionaries found themselves was recognized by Paton as a trying one. Being aliens, they could not engage in open political activity. Yet he believed that it was possible for them to show sympathy with the objectives of the national movement without overstepping proper bounds. Missionaries who were citizens of the ruling power had a greater freedom than aliens and should, he believed, speak out against all cases of gross injustice. There were, of course, many missionaries who would not have followed Paton in his sympathetic outlook on national activity. But his writing and the decisions of the international missionary conferences make it clear where the leadership of the missionary movement stood.

If the attitude of the missionary leaders was generally favorable, the attitude of the indigenous Christian leaders to the new national consciousness was vigorously affirmative. There were, of course, many indigenous Christians as there were many missionaries who were not so favorably inclined.

But most of the responsible representatives of the Asian churches, men such as Bishop Azariah and K. T. Paul in India, were deeply imbued with national feeling. Paul, who was general secretary of the Indian Y.M.C.A., took as his great goal the creation of an India that would be free, united, and true to her best traditions. He believed that the desire for this was from God. He made a great contribution to the life of the nation through the development of rural improvement centers. He also organized lectures on national questions that earned him the charge of "sedition" from the foreign community in India. He finally resigned the secretaryship of the Y.M.C.A. in 1930 in order to devote himself fully to the national struggle, but he died shortly thereafter at the age of fifty-five. Mahatma Gandhi, with whom he attended one of the Round Table Conferences in London, described him as a "thorough nationalist."

PRESENT ATTITUDES

In more recent years, since the new nations have been established, the discussion of issues related to nationhood has become more extensive and more complex. The general evaluation of national existence continues to be positive. "Nationalism in Asia, in contrast to the West," says an East Asia Christian Conference report, "must be regarded as a positive, integrating rather than a disruptive force." [5] The Nasrapur Conference of Indian Christians in 1960 declared that "Christians, if loyal to their faith, should be fully involved in the nation's concern to be truly a nation, exercis-

[5] East Asia Christian Conference, Kuala Lumpur, 1959. "The Witness of the Churches Amidst Social Change," in *Religion and Society*, Vol. VI (1959), No. 2, p. 30.

ing its vocation as a nation among nations, and safeguarding its integrity against disruptive forces from within or without." [6] African churches have now joined their voices to those of Asia. The Blantyre Synod of the Church of Central Africa (Presbyterian) stated in 1958 that nationalism could be a great force for good if it were harnessed and not looked upon as something to be feared.

The same attitude has characterized missionary bodies in the West in their evaluation of national consciousness as seen in the emergence of the new nations. The Church of Scotland General Assembly published a statement in 1959 saying, "We trust that the over-all policy of the United Kingdom government is not to discount and submerge nationalist sentiment. Nationalism is afoot all over the world. It can alternatively be judged sympathetically as essentially the awakening of a people to a consciousness of their human dignity or it can be written off as sedition. If the latter judgment stands . . . racialism is inevitably engendered. To sow the wind is to reap the whirlwind." [7] Among missionary leaders of the West the greatest attention to the questions raised by nationality has been given by M. A. C. Warren, former secretary of the Church Missionary Society of the Anglican Church. He has written about "nationalism as an international asset," [8] pointing out that each people is chosen by God for some task, but that the accomplishment of that

[6] Devanandan, P. D., and Thomas, M. M. *Christian Participation in Nation Building*, p. 295. Bangalore: National Christian Council of India, 1960.

[7] Church of Scotland. *First Report of the General Assembly's Committee Anent Central Africa*, May, 1959, p. 30.

[8] Warren, M. A. C., "Nationalism as an International Asset," *International Review of Missions*, XLIV (1955), p. 385. See also his book, *Caesar, the Beloved Enemy*. London: S.C.M. Press, 1955.

task awaits the assertion by a people of its individuality. This assertion, he says, is nationalism. Internationalism is not the negation of it but rather its fulfillment. The community of nations into which each brings its contribution can only be realized when each has asserted its own individuality.

Among the contemporary Christian leaders of the new nations the outstanding thinker about nationhood and all that it means is M. M. Thomas of India. Thomas believes that the national spirit has performed a great service in awakening the Eastern peoples, in shaking them out of their static societies, and bringing them with a rush into the stream of world history. It has pushed men up against fundamental questions about their existence as free persons; about society in relation to justice and love; about the historical process and its ultimate goal; about the world and its reality and meaningfulness. As national life brings men up against these issues, Thomas sees it as "an essential preparation of Asia for the gospel." This is not to say that men will accept the Christian answer to these questions, but the issues that nationhood raises are issues related to the message of Christ. The direction in which the national movement points as it struggles for justice and liberty, he believes, is the direction that leads on to the love and freedom found in Christ.

"HIS TRUTH IS MARCHING ON"

The contemporary thinking both among missionary leaders and Christians of the new nations betokens a more God-centered interpretation of nationhood than was given in the past. Christians see God as acting and ruling in the national revolutions, throwing down the pride and oppression of the past and raising whole nations to responsible life. "To Christian faith it is apparent that in the national revolution of our country God has been at work," declared the Nasrapur Conference in India. "If the Church is to have a right response to the life of the nation, it is necessary for it to discern the presence and work of Christ in Indian nationalism, broadly defined as the inspiration for the nation's struggle for its selfhood." [9] The same interpretation can be seen in Africa. N. Sithole in a book on African nationalism describes nationalism as the rejection of a rejection. White men have long rejected the African through the attempts they have made to dominate him and to divide society on racial lines. Now African nationalism is casting off that domination and that division of society—in short, it is rejecting the rejection—and in so doing is fulfilling one of God's purposes for man.

Today, as in earlier times, the mass of Christians in the new nations includes many who are more fearful of national existence than the statements of these leaders and church bodies would lead one to suppose. They fear that they will find themselves in some continuous inner conflict between their participation in the national community and their Christian faith. The emphasis upon God's purpose for the national existence and his action in the present sweep of national revolts is precisely the emphasis needed to overcome these fears. If God has a will for these peoples, if he is raising them through nationhood to face the issues of responsible life, then it behooves Christians to participate fully in the national community. They have no justification

[9] Devanandan and Thomas, *op. cit.*, pp. 294-295.

for holding worriedly aloof. Nasrapur went so far as to say that "if a Christian is either indifferent to or ignores this responsibility he is denying Chrst." [10]

The attitude toward nationhood can be seen affecting the whole way in which Christians of the new nations understand the Christian faith. Many of them are impatient with one of the principal directions of thought in the European and American churches, the direction that emphasizes how far God stands above the confused and sinful world of men. That brand of thinking in their opinion leaves human affairs all too much in the dark, with very little to choose between the best and the worst of human activities, between the dominating force of empire and the freeing force of nationhood. M. M. Thomas describes himself as "fed up with the one-sided attention to the religious ultimates which leaves Christians with no understanding of the Christian significance of the 'human.'" Christians in the new nations believe that human values are given by God and that the nation is one of those values. God made men in such a way that they would find relationship in nations as well as in families.

A STIFF-NECKED PEOPLE?

Danger lurks in the claim that God is at work in any particular movement—the danger of identifying that movement with God. The national movement obviously carries this danger. Though God may be at work in it, man's selfishness and pride are at work there, too. The nation may be part of God's creation, but that does not mean that everything the nation does is in accord with God's purpose. The

[10] Ibid.

Christians of the new nations are keenly sensitive to this danger. After all their positive evaluations of nationhood they are careful to append a word of warning. The World Council of Churches' conference on rapid social change held in Thessalonica, Greece, in 1959, where nearly half the participants were from the churches of the new nations, provided a fair example of the positive statement followed by the warning. The conference first affirmed the values of independent nationhood, saying:

Responsible participation in social and political life can only be achieved where each national group or unit can express itself in freedom. Therefore these nationalisms [of the new nations] should not be equated with that aggressive nationalism which seeks to dominate other peoples or an isolationist nationalism which denies responsibility for other people.

But then the participants added immediately:

Nevertheless it is necessary to be clear that even a legitimate movement of nationalism expressing the urge for political freedom or for nation-making has in it the seeds of perversion.[11]

They then went on to delineate the possibilities for idolization of the nation as the agent of total human redemption or else identification of the nation with certain traditional values or groups of people. They concluded that the church's participation in nationalism must be "positive" but also "critical."

This combination of appreciation and watchfulness could be paralleled from various other Christian groups in the

[11] World Council of Churches International Ecumenical Study Conference, Thessalonica, Greece, 1959. *Dilemmas and Opportunities, Christian Action in Rapid Social Change*, p. 57. Geneva: World Council of Churches.

new nations. The Bangkok Conference of 1949 said much the same thing, as did the speakers at Ibadan in 1958. N. Sithole in writing on African nationalism makes very clear his opposition to the brand of nationalism that thinks that everything the nation does is right and everything its opponents do is wrong. He wants no rejection of white men but only of their domination and exclusiveness. M. M. Thomas believes that in the Indian church God "is preparing a people who can discern what is of God and what of man's rebellion in the movement of national reconstruction." [12] And just because there is rebellion, pride, and self-seeking in the national movement requiring judgment within it, he argues that the church must relate itself more than ever to the national stream of life.

Not all Christians escape the dangers of nationalism. Nnamdi Azikiwe, who in October, 1963, became the first president of Nigeria, has spoken of the "God of Africa" as if this were a different God from that of the rest of the world. Colin Morris, the stormy petrel of the Rhodesian church, has told how when he was making speeches in opposition to a stand taken by the Nationalist party, he was condemned by local church elders for interfering in politics. When he asked them why they had made no such complaints during the four years he had been attacking the Europeans for their treatment of the nationalists, he was told that in those days he was preaching religion, not politics, because he was speaking for African rights. There are doubtless many who in this simple way identify the national cause with the Christian religion.

[12] Thomas, M. M., "Indian Nationalism: A Christian Interpretation," *Religion and Society*, VI (1959), No. 2, p. 14.

Even among the more sophisticated leaders of the church national blindness is not always overcome. When the Asian churches gathered at Kuala Lumpur in 1959, they found to their distress that the divisions of opinion among them on international questions corresponded almost exactly to the divisions of opinion among their national governments.

"GROW OLD ALONG WITH ME"

Their difficulty points ahead to the greatest problem that arises following national independence. It is the problem of bringing together the independent states and finding ways whereby they can settle their differences and work together rather than fighting one another. With this problem the new nations join the old nations. Europe and the Americas are as concerned to find a solution as are Asia and Africa. Thus far the Christians of the new nations have been too engrossed with the unfolding issues of national existence to do much thinking about the problems of international existence. In this they are typical of most of their compatriots. They are just discovering what it means to be a nation and to be responsible for their own life in the world rather than to follow the orders of imperial masters. National sovereignty means to them the freedom to make the choices of their own destiny, and they have been totally involved in those fateful choices.

But already the international problems press in and, along with the peoples of the West, they are being forced to realize that unrestricted national sovereignty for many nations may mean chaos for all. Asian Christians gathered at Pematang Siantar in Indonesia in 1957 recognized that "the newly independent countries of Asia are only beginning to realize their nationhood . . . at exactly the historic moment when national sovereignty is being called into question." [13] They must indeed affirm the value of their own national independence, but they must be ready to move forward from that to explore new forms of national interdependence. The Nasrapur Conference concluded its statement on nationhood with the reminder "that national sovereignty is not an ultimate goal. Already the nations are pressing on in the search for new forms of international relationships based on the growing interdependence of nations. The purpose of the living God in history is never static." [14]

So new horizons are opening. The positive attitude toward nationhood, even when combined with a wary glance at the dangers of nationalism, is not the end of the road. All the problems of life in the world of nations loom ahead. Only it must be clear that the new horizons lie beyond and not short of nationhood. The new ways of international existence, whatever they may be, must preserve the sense of responsible life that nationhood has brought. Among the churches of Asia and Africa there is to be no backtracking on the support for national existence that has characterized the main line of their thought ever since the national movement was born. There must be no withdrawal from it, but there must be readiness to go beyond it. "The purpose of the living God in history is never static."

[13] Asian Christian Study Conference, Pematang Siantar, 1957. *The Social Goals of the New Asia*, p. 27. Geneva: World Council of Churches.

[14] Devanandan and Thomas, *op. cit.*, p. 297.

3

NATIONAL CONSCIOUSNESS ENTERS THE CHURCH

Not from some Olympian height have the churches watched the national spirit seizing and shaking the traditional societies around them. They are part of those societies, and they, too, have been shaken. National feelings have colored the warp and woof of their life, and they have had to face the question that confronts Christians everywhere in the world: What place should national consciousness have in the church of Christ?

Sometimes it has a sorry place. National feeling can build up the walls that Christ broke down so that one part of the church becomes completely isolated from another. In our own time in North America there are those who would make the church an appendage to the national effort in the world struggle. They raise bitter protests whenever their church is associated with sister churches in unfriendly countries. This kind of national feeling inside the church, regardless of the country in which it is found, can twist and misshape the response that the church makes to the Word of God.

And yet there is a sense in which national consciousness has a helpful—one almost might say essential—place in the life of a church and in its response to the Word of God. That Word is no external set of rules that can be accepted without being appropriated. It is a personal Word addressed to each Christian and to each body of Christians. Therefore, each body of Christians, like each individual, must make its own response. It cannot exist on the basis of other peoples' beliefs and other peoples' teachings. It must be answerable for its own life and must do its own thinking and preaching. It should, indeed, share its thought and preaching with other parts of the body of Christ since the church is one throughout the world. But the sharing can be no excuse for a parasitical existence feeding on the convictions of other Christians.

As each part of the church makes its response to God, it must do so in terms of its own situation. A sense of the community in which it is set is therefore an essential element in the response. National consciousness is just that sense of the large community in which the church is set. With the growth of national consciousness a church becomes more aware of where it is placed and of the body of men for whom it is responsible. Thus a certain national consciousness is necessary if a church is to be aware of its particular identity and to lead a responsible life before God.

It is no accident that since the coming of national independence the Christians of Asia and Africa have begun to speak about the selfhood of the church. The most recent assemblies of Asian and African churches have heard major addresses dealing with this theme. Dr. E. Bolaji Idowu, addressing the All-Africa Conference of Churches in Kampala, Uganda, in April, 1963, pointed out that selfhood will not come automatically to a church any more than to a person. It requires autonomy and the exercise of a will of one's own. "The Church as an autonomous being should have a will of her own which is brought to bear upon every decision relating to her life and mission," he said.

NEW CHURCHES FOR NEW NATIONS

If all this is true, then it is proper to create autonomous national churches within the different nations so long as they remain in full fellowship and communion with one another. The creation of such churches has in fact been the most obvious counterpart in church life to the growth of national consciousness. In the West autonomous national churches appeared with the Reformation, though national identities had often interjected themselves into church affairs before that time. In Asia and Africa such churches have come into being as their communities have become conscious of a national identity. Already at the beginning of the twentieth century new national churches were starting to emerge in the colonial lands of Asia. There was even a small forerunner in the late nineteenth century, the so-called "National Church of India" established by a nationally minded Christian in South India in 1885, the same year in which the Indian National Congress was formed. But this was more a movement than a church, since it brought together leading Indian Christians of several denominations and advocated the recognition of national saints from all communions. At the turn of the century the Roman Catholic Church experienced a great national revolt in the Philippines, which resulted in the formation of the large Philippine Independent Church. Among Protestants, what may be regarded as the first national church in the colonial lands, a body governing itself, bringing together people from all over a nation and having a distinctly national interest was the Presbyterian Church in India established in 1904 by the union of Presbyterian bodies from all over that country. On the same pattern the Korean Presbyterian Church was established in 1907.

With the growth of national consciousness following the First World War independent churches began to shoot up all over Asia. In India there emerged within a year after the war the Tamil Evangelical Lutheran Church and the Gossner Evangelical Lutheran Church. The larger Andhra Evangelical Lutheran Church followed in 1927. In 1922, the largest of India's non-Roman bodies, the old Church of England in India, changed itself into the Church of India, Burma and Ceylon, taking on a national form and soon giving up its ties with the imperial government. After the division of India and Pakistan, it became the Church of India, Pakistan, Burma, and Ceylon. In Korea the Korean Methodist Church was established in 1930 as the one independent church growing out of the work of American Methodism in the new nations. The great churches of Indonesia were organized as independent bodies in the 1930's as national consciousness became stronger in their land—the Batak Church in 1930, the Minahassa Church in 1933, the Moluccan Church in 1935 and the Timor Church in 1937.

The same transformation took place in Africa following the Second World War. The largest non-Roman ecclesiastical body in Africa, the Church of England, began to form autonomous provinces in 1951 and completed the process a decade later. Provinces were set up in succession for West Africa, Central Africa, East Africa, and Uganda. In the smaller denominations a similar process took place. The Presbyterian Church of the Cameroun, for example, broke off from its American parent body in 1957. In describing this general change in Africa as well as Asia, we should note that for congregationally organized denominations the shift to a national structure was not so marked because they were more locally oriented from the start. The Burma Baptist Convention, for example, was organized in 1865 almost a century before the more recent African churches.

The emergence of national churches was not without its tensions. Traditional ties with the West came into conflict with new national enthusiasms. In India the Indian Christian Association, which had been founded for dealing with the social and political problems of Christians, fell during the 1930's under the influence of a bitterly antiforeign faction, who not only criticized all foreign leadership but also wrecked the association by denouncing those Indians who cooperated with foreigners. In the quieter days since independence an Indian Christian looking back at those troubled times has commented that the "revolt was characterized by a violent and somewhat unreasoned criticism of everything that the missionary said or did." [1] In Burma, during the same period, Burman Christians demanded complete freedom from missionary leadership and threatened to refuse to ac-

[1] Ecumenical Study Conference for East Asia, Lucknow, India, 1952. *Christ the Hope of Asia*, p. 18. Madras: Christian Literature Society, 1953.

cept any more missionaries unless mission funds were turned over to the control of the indigenous churches.

"A HOUSE DIVIDED . . ."

In a few places, as the national spirit took hold, the strife became so intense that the church was split. The most extensive rupture in Asia occurred in the Batak Church in Sumatra, one of the two largest Protestant churches of Asia. In the 1920's and 1930's, continuous ferment prevailed against foreign missionaries. The Batak Christian Association, an essentially political movement, was formed in 1917 and caused much unrest for a period of years until the government imprisoned its leaders. But then the national feelings were brought into the church organization, and before long there appeared in the city of Medan a separate congregation calling itself by the title of "Mission Batak," with the ringleaders of the old association behind it. In 1931 this group led a strong independence drive in the churches and two years later the separatist party had seventy-five congregations as well as a teacher training institute and a home economics school. There were personal motivations in all this, to be sure, but the effective power of the divisive forces lay in their appeal to national pride. Today the groups that split off at that time have more than one hundred thousand members. They still have not been reconciled to the mother church, which is about eight times their size and which has had no foreign leadership for over two decades.

The most devastating effects of nationalistic splits from the church have come in Africa. A whole series of separatist groups have been founded in almost every part of the continent. They began in South Africa, where the church was oldest and its leadership most advanced, in the early years of this century. Bishop Bengt Sundkler, who made the most extensive study of these movements, reached the conclusion that resentment of the white man's domination and discrimination and the demand of "Africa for the Africans" were the most important factors in their appearance. Following the First World War these groups began to appear in the area of the new nations.

The most famous of these movements was that of Simon Kimbangu who appeared in the Congo. He did not originally call for a separate African church, but believed himself to be an inspired agent of God. However, some of the leaders who gathered about him were less moderate than he and carried on a violently emotional kind of preaching. When the government began to be worried about possible political implications and started to put restrictions on their activities, the movement took a more distinctly nationalist tone. Kimbangu was arrested and imprisoned in 1921. He told his followers to trust in God and not in him, and they managed to keep up an underground existence even though he was held continuously in jail till his death in 1950. Many of his followers, not surprisingly, became bitterly anti-white and anti-church, believing firmly in a God of the Blacks and singing hymns to the effect that: "We have the Kingdom. They, the whites, do not have it."

The most fateful of all the separatist nationalist churches were two that appeared in Kenya not long after Kimbanguism began in the Congo, namely the Kikuyu African Orthodox Church and the Kikuyu Independent Pentecostal Church. They were purely the result of rebellion among certain of the Kikuyu against white domination in the church and especially against the attempt of missionaries to forbid certain traditional customs. The two church bodies were closely linked with the Kikuyu Central Association, a political organization begun in the 1920's for recovering land from the white man, later headed by Jomo Kenyatta. Each of the churches began a school system following the practice of the missionaries' churches. The Orthodox group started the Kikuyu School Association, and the Independent Pentecostal group founded the Kikuyu Independent Schools Association. Their schools became the training grounds for nationalist leaders through the years. It was in connection with these bodies that the Mau Mau movement was developed. Their schools sometimes were used as centers for administering the Mau Mau oath, which was deeply offensive to the traditional religion of the people as well as to the great majority of Kikuyu Christians. The basic teaching of the churches became for many, according to L. S. B. Leakey, an anti-white doctrine, though the Bible and the usual prayer book and hymnbooks continued to be used.

As independence has advanced in the African territories and the restrictions that were felt in the past have been lifted, the number of separatist churches has grown. One hears of new movements springing up in West Africa, in East Africa, in Congo, and in the Rhodesias. Many carry bizarre names, such as the Sacred Society of Cherubim and Seraphim, which is perhaps the most prominent in West Africa. Since both nations and churches are advancing in independence, the appearance of new groups today is presumably due less to opposition to foreign control than it is to opposition to the traditional interpretations of Christianity and especially Christian discipline on matters such as polygamy. In the past, wherever foreign rule was more repressive these groups were more militant. It may be that with the withdrawal of foreign rule they will now be more peaceful and cooperative. Signs already point in this direction.

UNITY AND MISSION

The deep effect of national consciousness has been to create not splits but a greater unity in the church. This nationally inspired unity can be of two kinds. There is the unity that is more or less imposed on the church by direct pressure from the nation and the forces of nationalism. There is also the unity that develops from within as the church faces before God its responsibilities in the new nation. By and large the movements toward Christian unity in the new nations have been of the latter type. To be sure, there have been some indications of pressure from the nation for a greater unity in the church. An acute observer of the East African church scene writes that many of the leading Christians "see the division of the Church primarily as a threat to national unity." [2] President Sukarno of Indonesia made a plea to the churches in 1953 for religious unity in order to strengthen the Indonesian nation. In 1961 the military government of Korea ordered that each denomination have only one theological seminary. It refused recognition to the seminaries of the large schismatic groups that had broken away from their denominations. Thus the demand for national cohesion and order has become a force for church unity.

[2] F. Welbourn in *Essays in Anglican Self-Criticism,* edited by D. M. Paton, p. 60. London: S.C.M. Press, 1958.

But, except for a period of a few months at the end of Japanese rule in Korea, the new nations have yet to see any actual unifying of churches by government order such as happened in Japan during the last war or in Prussia early in the last century. The unifications that have taken place have come from the Christian desire to minister more truly to the nation. In the formation of the Church of South India, for example, the utmost concern was shown for a truer and more effective ministry to the nation, while straight national feeling was assigned no such primary role. If it had been otherwise, there would not have been the possibility for the Christians of India and foreigners to work together as effectively as they did in the creation of that church.

Again, if we look at statements made in lands where negotiations for church union have been going on recently, we see that concern for the nation and a sense of responsibility for it, rather than national sentiment *per se,* are expressed as the reasons for unity. A conference of the major church bodies in Ceylon in 1961 declared that a united church could act more effectively and with greater benefit to the nation than had the divided church. Negotiations for church union in Nigeria originated in a resolution passed by the African delegates in the Eastern Regional Section of the country's Christian Council; the action deplored their divisions as contrary to the requirements of evangelization of their people and the command of their Lord.

When national sentiment first appeared in the churches, it stimulated missionary activity even more than movements for unity. The first great wave of national feeling in

India, which came at the beginning of this century, was very largely responsible for the creation of the National Missionary Society in that country in December, 1904. One sympathetic observer of that time described this evangelistic society as an outlet "for the nationalistic aspirations of the Indian Christian." [3] The society continued to be a center of strong national feeling down through the years, using little in the way of foreign help or consultation and emphasizing indigenous methods of mission work. In 1912, it launched what became a nationwide interest in *ashrams* as centers for an indigenous type of Christian work. From its discussions also arose the Christo Samaj, a body that was dedicated to reconciling Christianity and Indian life.

National enthusiasm played a major role also in the advancement and support of the other two principal missionary organizations in the colonial lands, the Isan Enim Bolana of Madagascar and the Zending Batak of Sumatra. The Isan Enim Bolana came out of the old, independent Malagasy life, and hence it commanded a great loyalty and support for its missionary activity from nationally minded Malagasy. The Zending Batak enjoyed a wide popularity and increasingly abundant funds for many years because it was an indigenous movement free from foreign domination. It was, to be sure, very much a child of the German missionary statesman, Johannes Warneck, but he rightly foresaw that it would have to be so constituted as to appeal to the national sentiments of the Batak people.

[3] Popley, H. A., *K. T. Paul*, p. 50. Calcutta: Young Men's Christian Association, 1938.

DROPPING THE PILOTS

Another great positive effect of the national spirit is the stimulus that it has given to the development of national leadership in the church. When the national churches first were established as independent bodies, they were still inevitably dependent upon a large proportion of ministers and church officials imported, one might say, through the work of the foreign missions. Gradually this situation has been altered. The first large church in the colonial lands to break loose entirely from direction by the foreign missionaries who had founded it was the Gossner Evangelical Lutheran Church in India. The foreigners who had worked in that body were all Germans who were interned or deported by the British government during and after the First World War. The group of Christians that they left behind was made up of tribal peoples in the south of Bihar province. Nearby denominations with foreign leadership invited these people to join forces with them, but the group finally decided to organize its own church with its own leaders, which it did in July, 1919.

In other churches the demand for greater leadership by nationals grew apace—in Asia especially following the First World War and in Africa following the Second. The case of the Philippines is typical of Asia. The central body for the Protestant denominations there, originally entitled the Evangelical Union of the Philippine Islands, was at its start open only to American missionaries. This restriction was perhaps defensible in 1901 when the only Protestant church workers were the missionaries; it was indefensible when the national church began to grow.

Two years after the end of the First World War, the constitution of the union was changed to admit Filipinos. In
1929, the name was changed to the National Christian
Council, and missionaries were admitted only as they happened to be appointed by the national churches. Since the
Second World War all the chief leaders of every Protestant
denomination, except one, have been Filipinos.

If we look at the Congo, we may see how the same
process took place later and faster in Africa. The number
of Congolese ordained Protestant pastors was only five
in 1925, but was 336 in 1958. The increase in the number of ordained Congolese in the Roman Catholic Church
was even more spectacular, the first three being ordained
in 1937 and 460 of them being at work in the church
twenty years later. The Congo Protestant Council, which
grew out of meetings of the foreign missionaries starting
in 1902, was, like its Philippine counterpart, an organization made up only of missionaries. There was expectation
in 1932 that Africans would be admitted, but certain
conservative missions and government policies prevented
moves in that direction. Not till 1958 was the first official
African member seated. With the coming of national
independence in 1960, everything changed in a flash. The
constitution was basically modified so that the body became a council of national churches rather than of foreign
missions and Congolese were elected to the positions of
president and executive secretary.

In some countries the national government has thrown
its weight behind the movement to indigenize the church
leadership. India, after it gained independence, allowed no
foreigners entry into the country if they proposed to occupy

a position in the church for which a qualified Indian was available. More recently, in 1961, the government of Sekou Touré in Guinea has ordered that no Roman Catholic prelate could be accredited to the country unless he was an African. By now in Asia the transformation in the staffing and leadership of the church is fairly complete. In Africa there is still a long way to go, especially in the eastern and central parts of the continent. However, in light of the present temper of the African nations, there can be no doubt that the change will come about even faster there than in Asia.

There have been and still are many problems connected with this nationalization of the ministry and leadership of the church, not the least of which is the gigantic and slowly accepted task of training a ministry adequate to deal with the situations that the church must face. But there can be little doubt that the successful accomplishment of nationalization has been absolutely essential for the vitality and perhaps even for the continued existence of the church. If we would see what happens to a church that continues to depend on foreign sources for the supply of its ministry and leadership, we have only to look at the Roman Catholic Church in Latin America. In most Latin American lands that church, though it has been established for centuries, has failed to produce enough priests to care for its own members. The concomitant of this condition is that the church has lacked the strength to maintain and develop a vital life and witness of its own for that part of the world. The church was first established in a time of colonial dependence, and it has not yet fully outgrown that condition. The kind of dependent existence that has characterized the Catholics in Latin America might have been thought to be in store for all Christians in the new nations of Asia and Africa, since their churches, too, were established under conditions of colonial dependence. But the rise of national spirit in the churches and the forward thrust of national church leadership to a position of dominant influence and numerical preponderance has already made it clear that the churches in Asia and Africa—whether Roman Catholic or Protestant—will not suffer that fate.

One further impact of the national awakening is the interest that it has generated within the church in the national culture. The whole movement in the church to bring about a closer contact with the traditional culture has been more the product of national sentiment than of anything else. The Indian Christian writers who tried the hardest to "naturalize" Christianity in Indian culture with Hindu terms and Hindu analogies enjoyed their heyday at the time when the struggle for national independence was at its height. The greatest number of proposals for modifying Christian practice along the lines of African culture have come in the very years when African nations have been struggling to establish themselves. The first conference on Christianity and African culture was held, appropriately enough, in Ghana, then the Gold Coast, in 1955.

THE SILENT REVOLUTION

When we survey all that national consciousness has done, we are forced to conclude that it has been the strongest influence in changing the churches of Asia and Africa during the present century. This is not to say that it has been a stronger influence than the gospel itself. But the gospel has naturally been a force for continuity as well as for change in the life of the church. The most important development has quite rightly taken place where the impact of national consciousness and the impact of the gospel have coincided. This has been in the growing sense of selfhood in the churches. Churches that formerly thought of themselves merely as arms of European or American bodies, that looked to some foreign headquarters to make the decisions that affected their lives, have grown to the point where they know that they have a life of their own to live and a responsibility for themselves and their fellows. This change does not mean that they are isolated from other branches of the church, but it does mean that when they enter into relationships they do so with a sense of their own place and purpose. They know that they cannot be international without experiencing what it is to be national, just as a person cannot enter into relations with other persons unless he is himself. If he is not making decisions for himself and taking responsibility for himself, then it is not fully *he* who is entering the relations. In the appearance of church bodies that know themselves and their own responsibilities and thus can be related, if they so decide, to other areas of the church, we see the most important impact of national consciousness and at the same time a response to the address of God in Jesus Christ.

| 4

CHRISTIANS IN THE
NATIONAL STRUGGLE: ASIA

O GOD, save my country and save my soul!" These
words, according to the reporter of an earlier generation, constituted the first prayer uttered by Syngman Rhee
of Korea. Stretched out on the floor of a filthy prison into
which the light of day scarcely penetrated, with head,
arms, and legs chained down so that he could not move
for seven months, Rhee remembered the Christian teaching he had heard in school and accepted the Christian
faith as his own. He was in that prison because of his
leadership of the Independence Club, so in his Christian
belief he very naturally linked the needs he felt for his
country and the needs he felt for his own self—"save
my country and save my soul."

The prison cell stands as a reminder to us that in the
struggle for nationhood, as in everything else, it is actions
that finally count. We have looked at the attitudes of
Christians toward nationhood and at national feelings in

the church. But attitudes and feelings accomplish nothing till they lead to action. Christians who live by the action of God's love in Christ rather than by some attitude or feelings attributed to God should not need to be reminded that the best ideas and feelings are no substitute for acts.

What, then, have Christians actually done in the struggle of the nation to establish itself? The answer usually given is that they have done very little. The churches have been content to sit on the sidelines while the decisive battles for the nation were taking place. This common answer contains a measure of truth, but it is by no means the whole truth. Many Christians have been deeply and sacrificially involved in the national struggle. A symposium written in 1952 by a representative group of Asian Christian leaders declared that the majority of such leaders had "strongly supported the movement for national independence." [1]

Before passing judgment one way or the other, we should examine what Christians have actually done in some of the principal new nations, starting with those of Asia. It may be that when we consider the very small number of Asians who are Christians, we will feel that they have carried at least their proportionate share of the burden of establishing the new nations.

INDIA

India naturally comes first, since it was the country that took the lead in revolt against European rule. It also provides a good example of both Christian isolation and Chris-

---

[1] Manikam, Rajah B. (ed.). *Christianity and the Asian Revolution,* p. 86. New York: Friendship Press, 1955.

tian participation in the revolt. The church as such had little part in the national struggle. This was due partly to the fact that so many non-nationals exercised major influence in its governing circles. Also, as a body with primarily religious interests, the church felt that its chief concerns lay elsewhere. Yet, even if we should concede that the church's interests are to be centered on matters of religion—a disputable point from a Christian perspective—the church in India must still be regarded as showing a surprising degree of unconcern for the most burning issues before the men among whom it worked. One reads the church journals of the time when the struggle was at its height and finds only the palest and most minute reflection of the fires that were then consuming the land.

However, there were at the same time Christians who were vigorous representatives of the nascent nation, and their actions must be set against the common inaction. When Indian nationalism first took organized form in the Indian National Congress, Kali Charan Banerji, a Christian from a noted Bengali family, played a significant part in its development. In South India, where the oldest and largest churches existed, there appeared at the beginning of the century a nationally minded bloc of Christians, including the brothers-in-law, V. Chakkarai and P. Chenchiah. These men were concerned to make the church more aware of the national life and culture and used as their vehicle of expression a paper bearing the revealing title of *The Christian Patriot*. The Y.M.C.A. proved to be an early center of national endeavor and out of it came ardent patriots such as S. K. Datta and K. T. Paul.

From the beginning, Christians as a group stood against

any religious communalism or separate electorates and rights for the various religious groups. They threw their weight in the direction of a unified nation with common national institutions and equal rights for all, whatever their religion. The Indian Christian Association, formed in the United Provinces in 1892, regularly over the years denounced communalism and communal representation. Pandit Nehru, a dozen years before independence, spoke of the way in which Indian Christians had repeatedly condemned communal electorates and all other attempts to split up the nation. This unifying effort may be regarded by some as only a policy of expediency on the part of a religious minority too small to stand alone. But they should note that the Sikh community, which constituted an even smaller group, was talking in terms of guarantees and special rights up to the time when the British Parliamentary commission came to India to work out the final terms of independence. The Christian representatives before that commission reiterated their desire for a united nation with no reserved rights or privileges for any religious group.

THE GANDHIANS

The role of religious communities in relation to the developing Indian nation became more critical after Mahatma Gandhi gained the ascendancy in the National Congress. Gandhi's role was paradoxical in this regard. On the one hand, he was the first nationalist leader to touch the hearts of the Hindu masses and to relate himself powerfully to their deep religious feelings. On the other hand, he was acutely aware of the need to rise above any one religious community and to bind all religions together for the national welfare. He did his utmost to spread toleration and good will among the followers of the major faiths. He regularly included in his daily worship services, which were also his most regular public appearances, the scriptures and prayers of the various faiths. His way of binding the religions together was distinctly Hindu, assuming the basic unity of all faiths and worshiping with all as if there were no crucial decisions to be made in matters of faith. Thus even his most sincere efforts at religious unity were a type of Hindu imposition upon the situation. Christians would have been more inclined to press for brotherly actions between religious groups on the basis of God's will for men as we know it in Christ rather than on the basis of any assumed ultimate agreement in matters of faith.

The Gandhian movement captured the imagination of a considerable number of Indian Christians. Some of them gave notable service under him, particularly in his constructive program. There was Rajkumari Amrit Kaur, later the Health Minister for independent India, who came from a princely family in the Punjab but discarded her finery for the Gandhian homespun and traveled up and down the country with the Mahatma as his secretary. There were the Kumarappa brothers, J. C. and Bharatan, from an old Christian family of South India, who gave up important intellectual careers, one to become the director of Gandhi's Village Industries Program and the other to serve as a writer and publicist for the Gandhian cause and assistant director of the Village Industries Program. There was E. W. Aryanaykam who became the leader of the other main branch of Gandhi's constructive program, the Basic Education Movement, and laid the foundations for the Basic Education program of independent India.

All of these leaders espoused the Gandhian outlook on religion, often preaching and writing about the basic unity of all faiths and the impropriety of evangelistic work. All felt themselves alienated from the church. It would be hard to say whether this alienation was due more to their involvement in the national movement from which the church stayed apart or to their Hinduized religious positions. Certainly they felt that it was because of the former reason; in their own conception their outlook on religion was the truly Christian one.

These were the best known Gandhian Christians, but a considerable number of other Christians devoted themselves to the national effort and suffered imprisonment for it. There were also well-known figures such as Dr. H. C. Mukerjee of the University of Calcutta, who did not actually join the Congress party till after Gandhi's death but who was always a nationalist. He traveled widely as secretary of the All-India Council of Indian Christians, increasing the national consciousness of his co-religionists. After independence, he served as vice-president of the Constituent Assembly of India and as governor of the state of West Bengal.

THE MISSIONARY CONCERN

The bulk of missionaries, being foreigners with primarily religious concerns, stayed apart from any political involvement. Some were openly hostile to national agitation. A. J. Appasamy, the South Indian bishop, has stated that missionaries prevented the people whom they had gathered into the church from taking part in the struggle of the National Congress.[2] But there were also many who were sympathetic to the national cause. Some were outspokenly so, such as Rev. Ralph R. Keithahn, an American Congregationalist against whom the district magistrate of Madura raised objections for his alignment with nationalism and who was ejected from the country for a time. Four American Methodist missionaries were deported for nationalist statements at the time of the Second World War.

The best known missionary associated with the national movement was the Englishman, C. F. Andrews, a close companion of Gandhi's and a champion of the Indian cause during most of his life. He wrote a booklet in 1920 entitled *Independence—the Immediate Need.* He paid visits to South and East Africa, Fiji, and the West Indies to examine the lot of the Indian indentured laborers who were taken to those lands. He was to a considerable extent responsible for the success of the campaign to put an end to the indenture system for Indians. He was also closely associated with Rabindranath Tagore and his famous university of Santiniketan. After Andrews' death, a large sum was raised through Indian nationalist channels to found a hall of Christian and Western studies named for him at that university.

The government of India was concerned about possible unfriendly activity by missionaries and therefore made the decision to require from them a declaration of political neutrality. The decision was embodied in a controversial

[2] Appasamy, A. J. *The Christian Task in Independent India,* p. 4. London: S.P.C.K., 1951.

document entitled "Memorandum A." This was an agreement with the British and American missionary societies calling for a declaration of political neutrality from all non-British missionaries and including a statement of the intention of the missions to abstain from political affairs and to exert their influence, "in so far as it could be properly exerted . . . in loyal cooperation with the government of the country."

The requirement of the declaration of neutrality was later dropped, but the missions were nevertheless deeply involved with the British rule by virtue of the large grants for educational and social work that the government distributed. Mission schools and other Christian charitable enterprises were among the chief beneficiaries of these grants. They were, therefore, in the minds of the nationalists, appendages to the foreign regime. In an effort to escape some of the embarrassment of this connection, William Paton, as secretary of the International Missionary Council, secured a statement from the government in 1931 saying that the receipt of grants did not imply "any obligation actively to share in propaganda in support of the government" so long as the previously mentioned "loyal cooperation" were kept in mind. Such a declaration could not prevent the Christian schools and colleges from being among the targets chosen for attack whenever the National Congress determined upon a campaign of noncooperation with all government activities. Student strikes and mass demonstrations threw mission institutions into a great deal of confusion and conflict periodically up until the time when independence was finally granted to the country.

IN INDEPENDENT INDIA

It was the earnest hope of nearly all Christians, both Indian and foreign, that when freedom finally came the relationships of the church to national life would at last be clarified and that Christians would no longer be tarred with the imperialist brush because of the presumed Christianity of the imperial overlord. To a very large extent this hope has been fulfilled. Educated Indians, who were formerly the people most suspicious of the church for nationalist reasons, have been much less inclined to question the loyalty of their Christian compatriots. The Prime Minister has more than once spoken of Christianity as one of the old Indian religions far antedating the period of the British connection.

But the accusation that Christianity is antinational is still to be heard from the ranks of the conservative Hindu nationalists. The most noted, not to say notorious, example of this was the report of the Christian Missionary Activities Enquiry Committee issued by the state of Madhya Pradesh in 1956. This committee tried to show that the Christian church was opposed to the national unity of the country. "Christian obedience" was interpreted as meaning obedience to a foreign power, dismissing the possibility that it might mean obedience to God. Other Christian beliefs and writings were equally misinterpreted. "As one reads the missionary literature," says the committee, "one comes across phrases such as 'colony of heaven,' 'in the country but not of the country,' 'historical community of the redeemed.' All these smack of extraterritoriality. . . . It appears to us that the missionary 'strategy' (a word which recurs frequently) is to detach the Christian Indian from his nation." [3]

Though such accusations elicit approval from the Hindu militants, they have not proved convincing to the bulk of the leaders of the country who are willing to make a place for all religions. Christianity has, by and large, been given real freedom in independent India. There have been occasional difficulties for Christian educational work and occasional restrictive legislation such as the law passed in one state, but since repealed, requiring all religious conversions to be registered before a magistrate. More significant restrictions have been directed at foreign Christians coming to work for the church in India. Many limitations have been placed on their entry and on the opening of new stations for their work. These restrictions, together with attacks like those of the Madhya Pradesh committee, remind everyone that after independence just as much as before, the church's relation to national consciousness must be an overriding concern.

KOREA

"The Land of the Morning Calm" has been the land of endless turmoil in this century. Nowhere else has Christianity been so deeply involved in the struggle for national existence. Three factors have combined to produce this involvement. First, Japan, the imperial power against which the national movement was directed, was not nominally Christian. Hence nationalist sympathies in the church were not so clouded over by public association of Christi-

[a] Report of Christian Missionary Activities Enquiry Committee, State of Madhya Pradesh, 1956, Vol. I, p. 144.

anity with imperialism as they were elsewhere. Second, the imperial power, unlike the European imperialists, repeatedly demanded a semi-religious expression of loyalty from the Korean people and hence ran afoul of the teachings of Christianity and forced the church to be a center of disaffection. Third, the church impressed people as a force making for national strength because it emphasized education, character development, and democratic values.

Because of these facts men of patriotic sentiment were drawn to the church from the time when Japan began to take over the country. It was not solely their opposition to the Japanese but a wider concern to see their country vigorous and progressive that moved them toward the church with a sense of personal need. The conversion of Syngman Rhee is a clear example of the combination. Rhee, as has been mentioned, became a Christian while in prison for his patriotic activities. When he was able to move about in the jail, he convinced several of his fellow prisoners of the truth of his new faith. A number of future leaders of Korean life became Christians in that jail, and a vital Christian church came into being there.

The missionaries tried to restrain the nationalist ardor of such converts. The foreign Christians were not merely neutral but actually discouraged nationalistic efforts. They counseled obedience and nonviolence when Japan took over the direction of affairs in 1904. They were followed in this by some of the most influential Korean pastors. A mission report of 1903 stated: "But for the influence of the Korean Christians in the north, and particularly of one man, . . . Pastor Kil, the whole region around Pyengyang, famous for its sturdy fighters, would have arisen in insurrection. But this wise Christian leader . . . with the assistance of the Christian church . . . turned the fury of the whole north, and delivered Korea from tremendous bloodshed." [4]

But in spite of such teachings the church became a great center of nationalist aspiration. It was the strongest organization left in the hands of Koreans. It included some of the most vigorous nationalist leaders, such as Baron Tchi-ho Yun, former vice-minister of education and leader of the struggle for constitutional government; Sangjai Yi, secretary of the Korean Emperor's Cabinet; and Syngman Rhee, of later fame. It carried on the largest educational program then in existence in Korea, and modern education was the great hope of those who wanted to lay the foundations for eventual independence. And the church was a natural focus for opposition to the government's demand that schoolchildren and others should bow before the picture of the Japanese Emperor on feast days. To many Christians this smacked of idolatry, even though the rulers were careful to explain that it was only intended as a sign of respect.

THE REFINER'S FIRE

Japanese actions against the church soon erected it as a symbol of national resistance whether the church leaders wished it so or not. In 1912 came the notorious Conspiracy Case when 123 people, including 98 Christians, were arrested and charged with a plot to assassinate the governor-general. They were tortured, and forced confessions were

---

[4] Wasson, Alfred. *Church Growth in Korea*, p. 70. Concord, N. H.: Rumford Press, 1934.

extracted from them, but at the end of many appeals all but six were acquitted. None who knew those six, among whom was Baron Tchi-ho Yun, believed there could be any truth in the charges. Three years later the six were released. In succeeding years came harassment of Christian educational work, the requirement that only officially prepared textbooks be used, and the demand in 1915 that within ten years all religion cease to be taught in school, a demand that was withdrawn in 1920. A government spokesman declared that "missions should leave all affairs relating entirely to education entirely in the hands of the Government. . . . Education must be decidedly nationalistic and must not be mixed up with religion that is universal." [5] The nationalistic quality that was demanded in the study courses of the schools had, of course, nothing to do with Korean nationalism.

The extent to which Christianity became identified with Korean national hopes was shown in the Independence Movement of 1919. At that time the most respected leaders of the Christians, led by the most famous of their ministers, Pastor Kil of Pyengyang, joined with the leaders of another nationally minded religious body, the Chondokyo, and issued a Declaration of Independence. The reading of this statement launched a tremendous nonviolent protest over the entire country against the Japanese rule. The government treated the affair as if it were essentially a Christian rebellion, rather than the spontaneous reaction of the whole people. A report issued by the Educational Affairs Bureau quoted a statement that "the mobs each time collected

[5] McKenzie, F. A. *Korea's Fight for Freedom*, p. 214. New York: Fleming H. Revell and Co., 1920.

at the churches and started from there." [6] Nearly all the pastors of Seoul, along with masses of Christians all over the country, were arrested, church buildings were destroyed, and Christians often indiscriminately attacked. Even the missionaries, who had taken pains to be neutral and knew nothing of the plans for the movement, were accused by Japanese papers of being at the root of the trouble. When the missionaries saw the atrocities inflicted on the people, they did protest vehemently, and their protests were heard around the world.

Thus Christianity entered the period between the two world wars already closely tied to Korean national aspirations. The Japanese policies of that period tightened the knot. As the Japanese militarists won increasing control of their country and moved toward war, they determined to establish their own nationalistic religious outlook firmly in Korea. Shinto shrines were erected all over the land. Schools and later churches were ordered to go through ceremonies before these shrines. The foreign missionaries for the most part opposed these moves vigorously, the Presbyterian Church, U.S., closing all their schools. Eventually all missionaries were forced out of the country. Korean church leaders resisted also, but they were subjected to a multitude of subtle pressures and attacks, which wore down their opposition. Christians who remained intransigent were thrown into prison. When necessary, votes approving the shrine worship were forced through church bodies under the watchful eye of the police with no opportunity allowed

---

[6] Nakarai, Koyoshi. *Relations Between the Government and Christianity in Chosen,* p. 31 Government-General of Chosen, Educational Affairs Bureau, 1921.

for dissent. During the years of the war the most severe pressure was applied. More than two hundred churches were closed, and some three thousand Christians were jailed, a good number being killed. The execution of a large number of church leaders was about to take place when the war suddenly ended.

BONDS IN FREEDOM

When freedom finally came to Korea, it was only natural that Christianity should be closely identified with that freedom and with the national life that emerged. The first president, Syngman Rhee, and a majority of his cabinet, as well as 25 per cent of the members of the national assembly, were Christians. Many Japanese religious buildings were taken over by the church, suggesting that as Shinto had been imposed by the imperial power Christianity expressed the free life of the nation. On the site of the chief Shinto shrine on a hillside overlooking Seoul, "the very place," as the churches stated it, "where the Japanese imperialists tortured our nation in general and the Korean churches in particular" [7] a Christian museum was established. There each Easter day twenty to fifty thousand Christians assembled for a sunrise service.

In North Korea immediately following the war the churches took a vigorous lead in resisting the Communists in the name of national freedom as well as religion. In each district the church led in the formation of "Self-Government Societies" or "National Establishment Preparatory Societies," which showed that there was to be no

[7] East Asia Christian Conference, Prapat, 1957. *The Common Evangelistic Task of the Churches,* p. 44.

easy acquiescence to the Communist rule. The first political parties were organized by pastors, the Social Democratic Party by Rev. Kyung-chik Han of Sin Wiju and the Christian Liberal Party by Rev. Hwasik Kim of Pyengyang. The executive committee of the first was arrested, and Mr. Kim and some forty leaders of the second disappeared after being imprisoned. The crucial public clash between church and government came, significantly enough, in connection with the celebration of the great nationalist anniversary on March 1, the date of the Independence Movement of 1919. The churches, because of the deep Christian involvement in that movement, organized great meetings for the first free celebration of that day in 1946. The government put these under an interdict and arrested most Christian leaders involved. Nevertheless some huge meetings were held, and, though some pastors were arrested on the platforms, crowds moved out from them through the streets shouting for freedom, waving Korean flags and clashing with Communist groups. After this the government worked quickly to organize a puppet "Christian League" and to jail Christian leaders who did not fall in with it. Masses of them were killed at the time of the war in 1950.

The March 1 celebrations also marked the beginning of open collision between Christians and Communists in South Korea. Both groups tried to seize the initiative on that occasion for "blessing the nation" as a Korean Christian writer, Yang Sun Kim, has expressed it in his *History of the Korean Church* (1945-1955). In his opinion it was the Christian triumph at this point that prevented the as yet unformed Republic of Korea from being taken over by the

Communists.[8] Though this may be claiming too much, the Christians certainly played a large part in the rejection of the Communist movement in South Korea.

In the South, therefore, there has been no such struggle with the government as there has been in the North. At one time only has there been any open clash between loyalty to the nation and loyalty to Christ. That was in 1949 when the Educational Department of the government demanded that schoolchildren bow to the flag. Forty-one Christian pupils were expelled from a public school because they refused. At once the old passions related to the struggle over bowing before Shinto shrines were aroused, and church spokesmen prophesied that the fate that overtook Japan would befall the Korean nation that followed the path of such idolatrous nationalism. The government quickly backed down, accepting a form of salute that was proposed by the churches.

There has, in fact, been so little tension between national life and Christianity in South Korea that it may be claimed that this is one country of Asia where the danger for the church lies not in too great isolation from the national struggle but in too uncritical identification with it. Here the dual attitude of Christianity toward the nation needs to be remembered.

The church was fully involved in the resistance to the Communist forces, which invaded in 1950. When suggestions began to be made for an armistice to put an end to that fighting, one group of Christians held a Christian Anti-Truce Convention in Pusan, sending out an appeal

[8] Kim, Yang Sun. *History of the Korean Church* (*1945-1955*), p. 37. (Mimeographed.)

to the churches of the world in opposition to any truce. The fighting brought further evidence of Christian solidarity with the nation in the development of a chaplains' corps by ministers of the church. This became an important factor in building up the morale of the soldiers. General In-kwun Chun in a testimonial to the chaplains' corps, whose establishment he had originally opposed, expressed the fusion of national and Christian ideals. He said: "No matter how dangerous the situation, the confident statement that God was with us made it possible to carry on normally, and it could be seen that the soldiers trusted their chaplains like their own parents. I came to change my formerly mistaken opinion of the work of the chaplains and to lean heavily on their cooperation." [9]

The extent of identification between the outlooks of the church and the nation has been evident also in the fact that the church has been quite as slow as the rest of the nation to reach out a reconciling hand to Japan and to Japanese Christians. While other Asian nations that were occupied by Japan have established friendly relations again and there have been frequent exchanges between their churches and the Japanese churches, the Korean nation and the Korean churches have stood aloof. Not till the 1960's was there even a beginning made of some significant contact between the Korean and Japanese churches. The North Korean Communists have shown far more readiness to forget the past in their relations with Japan than have the South Korean Christians. Relations between Chinese and Japanese Christians have been much more frequent and cordial than those between Korean and Japanese Chris-

[9] *Ibid.*, p. 39.

tians. Korean businessmen have had more regular contact with their Japanese counterparts than have Korean Christians. One must recognize in extenuation of all this that the Korean church was especially subjected to suffering under the Japanese rule and that anyone who proposes reconciliation today is suspect if he is one who showed the slightest degree of compromise with the Japanese in earlier days. But extenuating circumstances do not dispense with the problem, and the problem in the Republic of Korea is evidently quite the opposite of the problem in any other Asian land.

BURMA

The story of Burma's struggle for nationhood has been a complex and painful one. Christians have shared fully in both its complexity and its pain. There has been not only the difficulty imposed by foreign domination but also the difficulty arising from ethnic differences within the country. Present-day Burma, like most of the new nations, is made up of various peoples with their own languages. Among the Burmans as a whole there are eleven major language groups, though Burmese is the official language and the predominant people are those who speak this language, the Burmese.

Burmese were the leaders in the national movement, and among Burmese Christians the relation to the new nationhood was not very different from what it was among Christians in a country like India. Burma was governed as a part of India until 1935, and the nationalist ferment stimulated by Gandhi had its repercussions in Burma. As Christian schools were disturbed by the noncooperation movement in India, so nationalist strikes were launched against Christian schools in Burma in 1930 and thereafter. Politically minded Buddhist monks who served as centers of nationalist agitation led the attack on religious teaching in the Christian schools, and pupils were restrained from attending classes. As Indian Christians stood for a unified nation without special privileges for any community, so the Burmese Christians advocated a united Burma with no communal privileges. As in India, there were a number of Christians who became ardent champions of the nationalist cause but were somewhat estranged from the churches, so among the Burmese there emerged during the 1930's groups of eager young Christian nationalists who also felt themselves to be out of touch with the church as a whole. In later years, following the war, such young people organized the All Burma Christian Youth League, which took an active part in nationalist demonstrations and parades and refused to join the less militant church-sponsored youth organizations until a merger was finally arranged in 1956 in the United Christian Youth of Burma.

The most prominent Christian national leader in the 1930's was Ba Maw, a gifted but mercurial lawyer, who became the first prime minister of the country after Burma was separated from India. He continued in that post till 1939. The British jailed him during the war for his opposition activities but when the Japanese took over the country he was freed and served as the head of the government they sponsored from 1942 to 1945. During this period he renounced his Christianity in order to win support from Buddhist circles. In doing this he showed his politically opportunistic character as much as the weakness of his

Christian beliefs. Another example of the same qualities was given by Mahn Win Maung who fought in the Burma Independence Army on the side of the Japanese. He was chosen to be president of the country during the period between 1957 and 1962, but only after he had given up his profession of Christianity in order to embrace the Buddhist faith.

ALTER-NATIONALISMS

The loss of such politically minded Christians to Buddhism, however, has not been a serious problem in the church. The serious problems have arisen from the traditional ethnic loyalties found among Christians in groups other than the Burmese. The most important group has been the Karens, the largest bloc among the Christians of Burma. Though less than a sixth of the Karens are Christians, they have provided leadership for the group. It was the Christians who, according to a writer of the last century[10] gave a sense of dignity and self-respect to the subservient Karen people. This led on to a feeling of nationhood among them. The Karen National Association was organized in 1881 under predominantly Christian leadership. A proposal began to be put forward that the Karens should have a separate territory within the country of Burma where they would be responsible, under the British, for the conduct of government. Sir San C. Po, an outstanding Christian and the first Karen member of the Legislative Council, wrote a book on *Burma and the Karens* in 1928 showing why the Karens must be regarded as a distinct na-

[10] Smeaton, Donald M. *The Loyal Karens of Burma.* London: K. Paul, Trench and Co., 1887.

tion. He claimed that they ought to have a country of their own in the future and separate electorates in any constitutional reforms.

The Karens held back from Burman nationalism and were loyal to the government during the British period. They formed the largest part of the army under the British. When the Japanese occupied the country during the Second World War, Karen guerillas carried on a highly effective struggle against them. This alienated them further from the Burmese nationalists. The Burma Independence Army, which was fighting on the Japanese side, killed large numbers of innocent Karens in a series of massacres during the war years. This added fresh fuel to the long-smouldering resentment of the Karens toward the Burmese. When the war was over and the British government sent a committee to inquire into the arrangements to be made regarding independent Burma, the Karen representatives made the request that they be given a separate Karen British colony. This request was, of course, not a practical possibility.[11]

After independence came, there was considerable uncertainty among the Karens as to their future. Under the leadership of Ba U Gyi, a relative by marriage of Sir San C. Po, they organized a Karen National Union and a Karen National Defense Organization to protect their interests. They refused to participate in the elections to the Constituent Assembly of Burma because they were unable to secure satisfactory boundaries for a state of their own in the new country.

[11] Cady, John F. *A History of Modern Burma*, pp. 549-550. Ithaca: Cornell University Press, 1958.

ORDEAL FOR THE NATION

Disasters followed in quick succession. Within a few months of independence the Prime Minister and most of his cabinet were assassinated. Then began a series of insurrections from Communists and discontented elements in the armed forces and militia. Karens, like some of their compatriots, organized to protect their villages and settlements in the uncertain times. On Christmas Eve, 1948, military bands allied to the government broke into eight churches in one district and killed eighty Karens at their Christmas Eve services. Shortly thereafter the Baptist Mission High School at Maubin was burned and in various places including the capital groups of Karens were attacked and killed. Soon the Karen National Defense Organization was launched in full-fledged hostilities with the government forces.[12]

This insurrection, which was one of several going on at the same time, has sometimes been mistakenly called a Baptist insurrection, since Christian Karens are Baptists. In fact, Baptists and Christians of other groups were involved on both sides of the tragic struggle. Ba U Gyi was the principal leader of the Karens, and there were Christians as well as non-Christians among the Karen forces. On the other hand, the commander in chief of the national army, till he was relieved of his command by the government, was General Smith-Dun, a Karen Christian. He and most of the other top Karen commanders remained loyal to the national government as did numbers of the

[12] Tinker, H. *The Union of Burma*, p. 39. New York: Oxford University Press, 1957.

lower Karen officers in the army, though the government disarmed them. The hard core of dependable army units, which could be used by the government in putting down the multiple insurrections, turned out to be units officered largely by Chin and Kachin soldiers, many of whom were Baptists. When the Prime Minister's personal Burmese bodyguard deserted to the insurgents, he turned to a corps of Chin Baptists for his protection.

In the first weeks of the Karen insurrection the American Baptist Mission in Burma sent a letter to the Prime Minister pledging their obedience to the laws of Burma and promising to seek in every way to promote impartially the well-being of all the peoples of Burma "under the duly constituted government of Burma." They said it was their earnest prayer that Burma might "speedily be united." At the same time, the bishops of the Anglican and Roman Catholic churches gave a clear call to their people to be loyal to the government. The Burma Christian Council in its report to the Asian churches' conference of 1949 declared that the church should be a uniting rather than a dividing force in the nation. It expressed grave concern over the insurrection, which was bringing "certain unofficial elements of Christians" into rebellion. At first nothing was heard from the Baptist churches because they had no central authority that could speak immediately for all of them. But the Burma Baptist Convention at its first general meeting after the fighting started, held in October, 1949, declared that Baptist Christians would "seek to bring about the cessation of violence and fighting" and "to restore true peace and harmony among all races and sections of the population in the Union of Burma."

The declarations for unity and peace were not mere words. When fighting was imminent, efforts to prevent the outbreak were made by representatives of the Baptist and Methodist missions.[13] After hostilities began, several missions to the Karen headquarters were undertaken on behalf of the government, chiefly by Mrs. Ba Maung Chain, a daughter of Sir San C. Po, to negotiate a settlement. These efforts came agonizingly close to succeeding. For a week in April, 1959, the guns were silenced in front of the seminary at Insein while conversations proceeded. But Karen commanders who held large inland areas would not agree to the terms accepted by the principal leaders. The fighting was resumed, and gradually the government wore down the Karen power. The important cities that they held were taken one by one. In March, 1950, the rebel capital was seized. Later that year Ba U Gyi was surprised and killed in his jungle hideout, and the Karen army became limited to an insignificant remainder of guerrilla forces operating in the more inaccessible parts of the country. Those who were Christians kept their Bibles with them, and men whom they have captured have reported that they still sing hymns and read the Bible at their camps.

RECUPERATION

This bitter experience left its mark on Burman Christianity for some time. A Christian soon found that he must, as Dr. Pe Maung Tin told the East Asia Christian Conference of 1959, "prove his loyalty to Burma and show that he has not been de-Burmanized on becoming a Chris-

---

[13] Cady, *op. cit.*, p. 596.

tian." However, with the evidence of vigorous national sentiment among many Christians, the suspicions of the population gradually subsided. A number of statements in church periodicals since the time of the insurrection speak of the passing of the doubts formerly held regarding Christians. U Nu, so long the premier of the country, went out of his way to emphasize the oneness of the Christians with all Burmans. The churches have repeatedly expressed their desire for the unity and harmony of the various peoples of the country and their loyalty to the government and its principles. Public spirited Christian leaders have appeared among some of the other minority groups besides the Karens and have won public recognition for the contributions that they have made and the leadership they have given.[14]

The establishment of a military dictatorship in 1962 was motivated in considerable part by the desire for national unity. Under the new regime a supreme effort has been made to get all the insurgents back into the pathways of peace and to rally all Burman people of the various groups under the rigid control and forceful leadership of the army.

INDONESIA

"The twelfth province of Holland" was an appellation used in colonial days for Minahassa, the most solidly Christianized section of Indonesia. "Dark skinned Dutchmen" was a phrase sometimes applied to the Ambonese, the earliest Christianized people of the islands and the people to whom the Dutch turned for their most loyal

[14] Tinker, *op. cit.*, pp. 73-77, 400.

lieutenants in government and army. Both Ambonese and Minahassans as well as the people from the island of Timor belonged to the Protestant Church of the Netherlands Indies, the body that until 1935 was a state church and that continued as long as the Dutch were in power in the area to be subsidized by the government in all its operations. With such a background it is surprising to discover how fully Christianity has become related to and has found acceptance by the proponents of the Indonesian national movement.

To be sure, it is not from Christians living in Minahassa, Timor, or Ambon that the nationalist efforts have come. Java has always been the center of Indonesian nationalism, and it was the Christians who lived in Java, followed closely by the Bataks of Sumatra, who served as the link between Christianity and the national movement. In the East Java Church, as a recent study has shown, national sentiment was becoming strong in the early years of this century at the same time that it first took hold among people outside of the church. Young Christians from the outlying islands who went to school in Java during the 1920's and 1930's became strongly infected with national ideas, memorizing nationalistic poetry from European literature and evidencing enthusiasm for parliamentary government. Organizations of Christian students became centers where the national spirit was imbibed. No outspoken national feeling was permitted by the government; so all of their sentiment had to be kept secret or expressed only indirectly. There was none of the public turmoil that so upset Christian institutions in India, Burma, and Korea during the same period.

TO THE COLORS

When, twelve days after the Japanese surrender, Dr. Sukarno and Dr. Hatta proclaimed the independence of Indonesia, all of this pent-up feeling came spilling out. It was, at least in Java and Sumatra, as if a great emotional explosion had taken place, and the Christians participated in this as much as any people. Leaders like Dr. Johannes Leimena, Amir Sjarifuddin, and T. B. Simatupang, who had been close to Sukarno and the inner circles of the nationalist movement, stepped forward to rally the Christians to fight for the national cause. General Simatupang, a Batak, was called from a desk in the customs office to become the organizer of the Indonesian army. He remained its chief-of-staff for some eight years till political differences with the government forced him into retirement at an early age. Leimena with some other Christians organized the Christian political party, Parkindo, within a few months of the proclamation of independence, and used it as a means of rallying Christians behind the new nation as well as a means of protecting the interests of Christians in the new nation. He has been almost continuously a cabinet minister in Indonesian governments from the beginning. A revolutionary nationalist movement was also organized among the Christian youth of Java, especially in central Java where the nationalist forces first got control. Known as the PPKI (Indonesian Christian Youth Association), it was dominated by the more nationalistically minded Javanese. It has since become something of a competitor of church-sponsored youth groups.

The meteoric career of Sjarifuddin provided the strangest of links between the church and the nationalists. Converted to Christianity while in jail for early nationalistic activity, he became a typical young Christian Asian idealist. He corresponded with Toyohiko Kagawa whose Christian economic program in Japan had a powerful appeal for him, and he named one son Tito in honor of the nationalistic Yugoslav Communist. He held prayer meetings in his home regularly even when he was carrying the highest responsibilities in the country. He organized left-wing nationalist groups before the war and led the largest underground force when the Japanese came in. With the declaration of independence he stepped into the thick of the fray, inspiring many young Christians as well as others to join guerrilla bands and the armed forces. He was selected as minister of information in the first cabinet and then became defense minister, and in July, 1947, the prime minister of Indonesia. Disagreements over his attempt to negotiate an end to the fighting with the Dutch led to his fall from power six months later. He formed an opposition coalition, at that point becoming more closely allied with the Communists. Finally, in July of that year, he announced that he was a Communist. Few have felt that this announcement represented his honest convictions. Those who knew him agree that he was too much of a nationalist and too religious to be an orthodox Communist. But they also agree that he was exceedingly ambitious and easily influenced, and at that point it looked as if he might lose control of his coalition if he did not joint the Communists. His career came to a rapid end. There was a clash between some Communist guerrilla forces and the government, and he was captured. He was put in jail, and one night while a young Christian in charge of the jail looked on, government troops came with orders that he be handed over to them. They took him down the road and shot him.

During this same time the Batak Christians in Sumatra threw themselves wholeheartedly into the independence struggle. Local and regional church councils became, with simply a change of name, governing bodies for the revolutionary regime. The youth fought solidly against the Dutch reconquest of the Batak country in 1947-1948. Christian revolutionary leaders, such as Colonel M. Simbolon and S. Sarumpaet, served as ministers of the new government of Sumatra. For many Bataks as well as for Christians in Java the nation seemed to have become almost an idol, as their church leaders at the Bangkok Conference of 1949 feared. A reminder had to be issued by the chief officer of the Batak church that the freedom cry was not proper for church services.

NARROW PASSAGE

Among the Christians of eastern Indonesia—Ambon, Minahassa, Timor, etc.—the picture was very different. National consciousness seems to have been little developed up to that time among large sections of these people. Thousands of Ambonese in particular felt no sympathy with the national movement. They emigrated to Holland rather than live in an independent Indonesia. Some of their compatriots who stayed behind engineered the most violent of replies to nationalism in the so-called "RMS affair."

The motivating factor behind this affair seems to have been fear. The Ambonese saw Indonesian sovereignty recognized in 1949, and they feared this would mean persecution of Christians and the end of employment for Ambonese soldiers. So in April of 1950 their elected council in Ambon declared the independence of their area, consisting of five small islands, under the name of the Republic of the South Moluccas. (The initials for the Indonesian words are RMS.) The proclamation of the republic took place in the context of a Christian religious service, and there is no doubt that Christian sentiment in the area favored the move. The Church of the Moluccas, as such, took no stand in the struggle, remaining passive though full of tension. Its members were mostly "RMS" men, but it was long accustomed to obedience to government and it was closely tied to sister churches in other areas. Some of its pastors, however, were vigorous in support of the rebellion, preaching on such themes as "the children of light and the children of darkness."

At first the central government attempted to negotiate, sending Dr. Leimena as a cabinet minister who, though long a resident of Java, was himself an Ambonese. But the rebels refused to discuss the question of their independence. So later in the year Djakarta's forces attacked with an overwhelming superiority of numbers. The Ambonese had crack troops, but they were few. Bitter house to house fighting gradually drove them from control of the city of Ambon. The city and the country around it suffered heavy damage. The final blow was dealt by troops from Minahassa, showing the devotion to the national cause that was found in the church of that section. The RMS fighters withdrew into the wild and mountainous island of Ceram, and a few are said to be still holding out there. But the

Ambonese as a whole were forced to see that their future lay with the rest of the country. They were treated with generosity by the central government, which rushed in relief supplies. They have been eager to demonstrate their loyalty and national spirit in the succeeding years.

The years since the Moluccan revolt have seen one other major rebellion in which Christians have been heavily involved. This was the widespread revolt, aimed primarily against Java's dominance, that took place in the islands of Sumatra and Celebes from 1958 to 1961. Muslim as well as Christian areas were active in this at first, but the most stubborn resistance to the government finally centered in Minahassa and the Batak land, both Christian regions. A disproportionately large number of Christians took up arms, though it must be recognized that this was on the basis of regional and family loyalties rather than for their religion. The Batak and Minahassa churches officially tried to stay out of the conflict. They did not bless the rebellion, nor did they condemn it. With so many of their members taking part, however, they could not avoid a certain degree of involvement and a considerable degree of sympathy. They devoted their main efforts to reconciliation between the hostile forces and tried to serve both sides. Pastor Wenas, who had been the most vigorous spokesman for the independence of the church of Minahassa, became the chief mediator between the government and the rebels in this area, traveling freely through both lines and refusing the blandishments of both sides. The National Council of Churches at its meeting in 1960 refused to try to judge who was right in the conflicts that were causing so much distress to the people but called for a way out on the basis of repentance, love, and forgiveness. Eventually this policy of reconciliation without revenge became the basis for a settlement of the rebellion.

It should not be thought that because of these military struggles the Christians as a group have ceased to be strongly national in their outlook or have become unacceptable to the national leaders. After all, the most continuous irritation inside Indonesia has come not from Christian but from Muslim rebels, the Dar-ul-Islam force that is determined to set up a theocratic state. There has been no such explicit religious rebellion among the Christians. The church members have continued to be very much members of the nation. They have provided more than their share of national leaders, sometimes holding as many as a fifth of the cabinet posts and several governorships. The Muslim leaders of government have been eager to stress in public the patriotic role of Christians and the place of Christianity in the national life.

FOR JUSTICE AND PEACE

Yet at the same time church leaders have shown themselves ready to criticize national actions on occasion. Usually it has been a gentle criticism, to be sure, but sufficient to show that the church more than most institutions of Indonesian life has a loyalty above that to the nation. When Dutch personnel were subjected to difficult regulations and ejected *en masse* from the country, the churches endeavored to provide relief and reminded the government of the biblical injunction, "You shall not oppress a stranger." When Chinese traders were ordered out of all villages, the churches took exception to the government's handling of the matter and asked the government to receive a church delegation that would suggest ways of implementing Indonesian citizenship for the Chinese. When a nationwide campaign of hatred and war preparations was under way in connection with the West Irian issue, the National Council of Churches was bold to call for a calm approach and a peaceful settlement of the dispute while affirming the validity of the Indonesian claim. "We appeal to our government and also to the Netherlands government," they said, "that they soon may meet around the conference table, abandoning resentments and sacrificing injured national pride on both sides." As the situation worsened with the naval incident of January, 1962, where the chief Indonesian officers killed happened to be Christians, the National Council called on the churches to increase their efforts at reconciliation. It called on the government to give guarantees for the realization of the legitimate aspirations for development in West Irian. These appeals were little heeded, but the conflict was finally settled by negotiation.

The constant crises through which the Indonesian churches have passed have begun to produce in them a mature sense of identification with the nation. The churches see themselves now as a part of their nation, and yet they recognize a loyalty that stands above the nation and gives them a responsibility for all humanity.

We have taken a long look at four Asian countries and seen something of the ordeal through which Christians have passed as their homelands emerged into nationhood. There are other lands that we might investigate, but their story would only reinforce the conclusion already evident that the relationship of Christians to the national struggle in Asia has been an exceedingly complex one. Any suggestion that they have as a whole been isolated from the affairs of their nations is clearly not true. The place where Christians pre-eminently belong is in the midst of the most significant struggles of their time. Many Christians in Asia have been in that place.

5

CHRISTIANS IN THE
NATIONAL STRUGGLE: AFRICA

DURING the Second World War when all men's eyes were focused on the fighting in Europe and Asia, Bishop Newell Booth, Methodist bishop in the Congo, wrote a book that spoke in ominous tones of what was going on in a continent that was then the object of little concern, Africa. He referred to the African as a man who was "a stranger in his own country" because of the white man's control of the land. He declared that "fires are laid for a conflagration when a whole continent is kept under the control of outsiders." [1]

The war was no sooner ended than, with the return of the soldiers, the fires of African nationalism burst forth and swept the continent with the speed of flames blown across dry grasslands. In an instant the white ruler who had been so often revered found himself upbraided and scorned. Few,

[1] Booth, Newell. *The Cross Over Africa,* pp. 2, 27. New York: Friendship Press, 1945.

if any, had expected so rapid a fulfillment of the bishop's prophecy.

The church, which had been so deeply involved in the early nursing of national sentiment, was utterly unprepared for what happened. For the most part, the churches of Africa tended to be quietistic in their outlook, taking no part in public affairs and counseling obedience to established governments. The missionaries, who held a far more dominant role in the African than in the Asian churches, often exhibited a desire to hold back what they regarded as too rapid political change. As a result there has been a widespread discrediting of Christianity in the eyes of many Africans for whom the demands of nationhood stand as the paramount demands of our time.

This is not to say that the churches have been completely separated from the movement of national self-assertion. They have in not a few instances given it a vigorous support, which has been much appreciated by national leaders. Before examining in more detail the tensions that have developed between Christianity and the national movement, we should look at some of the evidences of cooperation between the two.

AFRICA FOR THE AFRICAN

The most inclusive piece of evidence comes from the All-Africa Church Conference of 1958, the first continent-wide gathering of Christians. The delegates to that conference, representing nearly all the major churches, gave thanks for those colonial regimes that had allowed their peoples to move toward self-government and urged such a policy for all the territories of Africa. At the same time a plea was made that as self-government was established the rights outlined in the Universal Declaration of Human Rights be guaranteed to all citizens. This statement gives good reason to believe that African church leadership as a whole has been strongly in sympathy with the goal of democratic nationhood for the peoples of Africa.

This sympathy exists in the missionary leadership as well as among the Africans themselves. Many missionaries were present at the All-Africa Conference, wholeheartedly supporting its action, and doubtless most of those connected with the major denominations on the continent would be in agreement with the position it expressed. Actually, the first man to give political importance to the African national idea was a missionary of the late nineteenth century, Joseph Booth, who wrote a book entitled *Africa for the Africans*. He and some followers in Nyasaland formed the African Christian Union "to unite together in the name of Jesus Christ such persons as desire to see full justice done to the African race and are resolved to work toward and pray for the day when African people shall become an African Christian Nation." [2]

In our own time some missionaries have become outstanding spokesmen of the African viewpoint. One thinks of Michael Scott who has been the principal champion, both in the public press and in the United Nations, of the peoples of Southwest Africa. Trevor Huddleston, author of *Naught for Your Comfort*, is notable for his writing and speaking on behalf of the Bantu of South Africa. With him should be linked the American missionary, Ray Phillips, who as long

[2] Legum, Colin. *Pan Africanism,* p. 22. New York: Frederick Praeger, Inc., 1962.

ago as 1930 wrote a book entitled, *The Bantu Are Coming*. It was a plea for the fullest development of the Bantu and an attack on the inequalities and injustices under which they suffered. In the Rhodesias there are men like Garfield Todd who, in 1953, gave up his mission work in order to become prime minister of Southern Rhodesia with the hope of establishing a cooperative interracial society. When those hopes were dashed and he was thrown from power five years later, he made himself a traitor in the eyes of Rhodesian whites by going to Britain and calling for British intervention. There is Colin Morris, the fiery preacher of the Rhodesian Copperbelt, whose sermons and political efforts on behalf of the African resulted in the desecration of his church by white vandals and made him one of the most controversial figures of the territory. In Southern Rhodesia white settlers have requested the government to deport certain American missionaries because they have been too close to the African nationalist cause. The government did imprison the Anglican agricultural missionary, Guy Clutton-Brock, at the time of the 1959 emergency.

"THE FIREBRAND CHURCH"

Nyasaland is the country where the church has made the most determined effort in support of African national goals. The Church of Central Africa (Presbyterian), the dominant Christian body in the country, has reported that many of its elders participate in the Malawi Congress, the nationalist political organization, and that all of its members share the legitimate political aspirations of the congress. In many villages the composition of the local church and of the local branch of the congress are almost identical, so that the church has been facetiously dubbed "the Malawi Congress at prayers." Actually, ministers of the church have refused membership in the congress in order to keep an independent political position, so the identification is not so great as is sometimes suggested. Nevertheless, when the congress was banned in 1959 a number of important church workers were imprisoned among its leaders. At that time a synod of the church took a public stand against the violence exercised by government forces as well as the violence of some congress followers.

Before that crisis the church had already expressed its opposition to the governmental structure against which the congress was protesting. Nyasaland had been brought into federation with the Rhodesias in 1953, and the people feared the white man's domination of the new structures, which might mean the permanent suppression of the vast majority. The Blantyre Synod of the Church declared that it was unanimously opposed to the federation. It gave the lie to propagandists who would belittle the unrest in the country. "It is untrue to say that this unrest is confined to the educated African; it is found in every village. . . . [The people] don't want . . . white domination, race segregation, and discrimination here. . . . The increase in special police activities . . . is creating contempt for the law. . . . Schoolchildren are questioned concerning their teachers. . . . Sermons are the subject of special police reports, reputations are viciously maligned, . . . no public meeting can be held without informers or detectives being present." [3]

[3] Church of Scotland. *First Report of the General Assembly's Committee Anent Central Africa,* May, 1959, pp. 16, 18.

In these stands the African church was consistently backed by the Church of Scotland, whose missionaries had worked with it from earliest days. When the federation was established despite the Scottish church's plea "that no scheme be adopted without the consent and cooperation of the Africans" that church assured the Africans of its "constant watchfulness and sense of obligation to do all in its power to secure the recognition of the right of the African to his own land." [4] This deliverance was made in 1953, and the frequent reports and statements of the following years went far toward carrying out the assurance given. The Scottish missionaries who worked in Nyasaland presented its case vigorously in Britain. One of them, the secretary of the Central African Church, was debarred by the federation government from returning to his work in Africa.

PROTESTANT PROTEST

Close ties between Protestant churches and national feeling have also tended to appear in those territories where the colonial power was Roman Catholic and Protestantism was therefore looked upon as a natural ally of nationalism. In the Cameroun the principal independence movement, the U.P.C. (Union des Populations du Cameroun), found vocal agreement and active support among the Protestants, whereas Roman Catholics were not allowed to espouse it openly. Even when the movement developed strong Communist connections and took to violence, Protestant pastors and teachers continued to help it, though the missionaries warned them against this. The repressive actions of the military forces against the nationalists were so extreme and

[4] *Ibid.*, pp. 2,3.

indiscriminate that the faculty of one Protestant school sent a protest to the government and interviewed the Prime Minister to secure an end to torture and executions without trial. The chief leaders of the Union des Populations du Cameroun were Protestants. They lost their lives in the violence, and the eventual leadership of the independent country for which they had struggled so desperately passed into other hands.

In the Congo there was no such clear connection between Protestantism and the national movement. This was partly because the church, like every other segment of society, was less politically conscious. It was also because the government insisted on missionary leadership over the church in order to keep it from becoming a center of African national feeling.

Traces of a special connection with the national idea were long apparent in Madagascar where the Protestant traditions inherited from the old Malagasy kingdom served as one focus of national sentiment during the French period. The Isan Enim Bolana, which we have already met as the nationally minded missionary society of the Protestants, was watched with special care by the French authorities and efforts to make that society into the structure for church union were frowned upon by the French. The long-time president of the Isan Enim Bolana, Pastor Ravelojaona, was elected in 1939 as the Malagasy representative on the French Overseas High Council in Paris. On the whole, however, Roman Catholics were quite as involved in nationalist agitation as Protestants. Both churches joined in a 1957 appeal for the release of the main political leaders of the country who had been held in France from the time of the revolt of 1947. After independence, when the leaders finally were returned, the Protestant churches organized a public welcome for them.

The clearest example of the linkage of Protestantism to national sentiment comes, as might be expected, in those areas where the colonial power has been at greatest pains to identify itself with the Roman Catholic Church, namely, the Portuguese areas. Here the Protestants have been frequently accused by the authorities of "denationalizing" the Africans, the term "national" being used for a Portuguese rather than an African sense of nationality. Roman Catholic missions have been regarded as "nationally" oriented. Protestant missionaries, even though they have generally refrained from any public criticism of the Portuguese rule in order to continue their work in the colonies, have from time to time found themselves in trouble with the government. Half a dozen British Baptist missionaries were publicly censured or ordered out of Angola by the Portuguese regime at various times prior to the troubles of 1961. When rebellion and savage retaliation broke out in that year, some officials blamed the trouble on Protestants. The rebels did not harm Protestant missions, but Portuguese settlers vented their wrath on Protestant churches and service institutions. In the Luanda area of the Methodist Church alone twenty-one African pastors were killed and many more were thrown into prison. Four missionaries of the Methodist Church were deported and held in jail in Lisbon. Large numbers of church members were shot down at random. These atrocities should not be taken as proof that the Protestant churches were in fact behind the nationalist rebellion. Protestant church leaders emphatically denied that they had any part in planning the revolt or that their followers participated in sizable numbers in the killing of Portuguese settlers. But events suggested that the nationalists looked upon Protestant churches as friendly to the people. Soon after the rebellion, the Methodist Board of Missions in America called for the extension of civil liberties and extensive educational and social reforms in Angola "so that the people may more adequately prepare to take their proper place with other peoples of the world."

ON THE ANVIL

Despite such widespread evidence of the positive links between Christianity and African national spirit, it is clear that over most of Africa today the church is in real trouble because of the new national feeling. African nationalists are for the most part disillusioned about Christianity. They feel that the church has not backed them up adequately and that the missionaries at the point of crisis have sided with the white man. Recent expressions of missionary support are regarded as conversion after the cause is secure. Everywhere the claim is repeated that Christianity was used by the white conquerors to soften the African for their rule. The radical younger leaders, according to a report by Louis Lomax, demand that people "think black." Everything white is wrong. "The Church has not played a proper role in African affairs," they say. "It has stood against us, with those who would enslave us. The church is on its last leg in Africa." [5] The word "missionary" has become a term of rebuke in many circles of Africans—as it is also for many white men in Africa. "The Church has become a symbol of the dis-

[5] Lomax, Louis. *The Reluctant African*, pp. 3, 9. New York: Harper and Brothers, 1960.

honesty of the West," writes the noted African intellectual Ezekiel Imphalele.

Why this estrangement? Why, in spite of the efforts of many Christians to keep abreast of the national struggle, is there this common feeling that the church is removed from it? No one reason can provide an adequate explanation. Doubtless first place must be given to the belief prevalent among Christians that the church should not be concerned about public affairs. This belief has been characteristic of a large number of the Christian groups, especially the non-denominational missions, that have worked in Africa. It has been strengthened in all groups by the fact that many of their leaders have been foreign missionaries who felt obligated to the political inactivity expected of all foreign residents. Ever since this tradition was established by foreigners, it has continued to be observed by many of the older generation of African church leaders, who find it natural to follow the missionary's example. They also have a strong respect for the authority with which they have been familiar, the colonial authority and that of the chiefs, and they are distrustful of the political agitators who disturb the common life.

This attitude of political indifference is, oddly enough, even more characteristic of the separatist churches where there has never been any missionary leadership and where there is even a vigorous tradition of opposition to missionary leadership and to the white man. There have been a few separatist churches that have been simultaneously nationalist movements. One was the church established by the Rev John Chilembwe, who was shot while leading an insurrection in Nyasaland in 1915. There have been others that were the precursors of nationalist movements. But for the most part separatist churches have turned their followers away from the affairs of this world in favor of a heavenly hope. Some have even forbidden their people to take part in politics, thus making them less nationally active than the people in mission-founded churches.

RECONCILIATION OR BETRAYAL?

The churches that work with foreign missions of course have a still greater disadvantage in nationalist eyes in that they maintain links with the white man. This will be a continuing reason for tension between Christianity and extreme African nationalism. Even when the churches are anything but quietistic in regard to political affairs they cannot, if they are truly Christian, avoid serving as a place where white and black work together and as a center for mediation between the two groups. Accordingly, African pastors are criticized because they work with white missionaries while nationalist organizations, even where white men could well be admitted to membership—as in the case of the United National Independent Party in Northern Rhodesia—prefer to limit admission to black men. The attempt of the Christian to keep in touch with races other than his own makes him lose contact with those who think in strongly racist terms.

Unfortunately the racial inclusiveness of the church has played a less noble role in areas such as the Rhodesias, where there has been growing white settlement. Generally the inclusiveness has not been sufficient to bring about integration of white and black congregations. Each group has kept to itself. But the inclusion of white congregations in the total organization of the church has dampened any forthright recognition of African viewpoints by the church as a whole. In the 1920's and 1930's missions in the Rhodesias frequently raised their voices on behalf of the Africans and were regarded as the exponents of African interests. By the 1950's when the great issue of the federation of the Rhodesias and Nyasaland was raised, the Rhodesian churches, contrary to those of Nyasaland, no longer stood out as the champions of African resistance. The missionary societies in Great Britain were far clearer in their stand against federation than were the churches of the area. And the churches varied according to the number of white settlers they included. The Methodist Synod in Northern Rhodesia called in 1958 for a wider franchise for Africans and a common role of voters for all races, though it held back from advocating a universal franchise. The Methodist Synod of Southern Rhodesia, however, simply approved the advances already made in the franchise law. The Roman Catholics were more outspoken than the Protestants. The Catholic bishops of Northern Rhodesia issued a pastoral letter in 1958 condemning the exclusion of Africans from political, social, or educational facilities available to white men. The failure of the churches and of many missionaries to make common cause with the African opposition to federation has, more than anything else, led to a general loss of confidence in the church by Rhodesian nationalists.

RESPONSIBLE PROPHETS

Beyond the political aloofness of many Christians and the interracial quality of the organized church, there is a third reason for the separation of Christians from African nationalism. This is the tendency, which seems almost universal in the church today, to advocate moderation in public affairs. Responsible attitudes are those that recognize the limitations of a situation and the legitimate claims of opponents. This kind of responsible approach does not go down well with the ardent leaders of African nationalism. They are men who see things sharply from their own point of view, and they are impatient of apparent limitations in the situation. Hence they tend to be strongly critical of moderate approaches stemming from the churches, and the churchmen are soon left behind in their political agitation.

This problem was demonstrated very clearly at the time of the 1948 riots in the Gold Coast, which proved to be the turning point for the independence movement for all Africa. Christian leaders, like all other leaders, were working toward eventual independence. But those who were most closely identified with the church were stressing the need for gradual development and the importance of keeping open the channels of negotiation with the British rulers. In their negotiations they did not want to do anything that would endanger the maintenance of law or the effective operation of the government services. Kwame Nkrumah came on the scene with a frank espousal of political agitation rather than negotiation and a defiant readiness to risk a complete collapse of government in order to get rid of the British quickly. Nkrumah's lieutenants had no scruples about making false charges against the British government, since they believed their charges were true in essence if not in the particular instance. Men closer to the church felt themselves more limited by the demands of truth. When the riots broke out, the political naïveté of many churchmen and the imperialist sympathies of certain missionaries were laid bare by an article on the meaning of Holy Communion that appeared on the front of the government information sheet that was distributed all over the country immediately following the riots. The article was written by a foreign missionary who had been asked by the government to do this in order to provide something to calm the populace!

The response of the leading churchmen as a group, it should be said, was far more politically mature than this. They issued a statement after some months on "Christianity and Political Development," which declared first that the Gold Coast had a natural right to self-government. They then went on to press for good and honest government and the eschewing of all violence. They made it clear that Christians could take different views on political affairs. This balanced document had an important role in showing devout Christians that they could indeed struggle for the self-government to which they had a right. Many who had been uncertain of the church's possible backing for independence agitation seized on this for support. But at the same time it was regarded as far too tame a statement by the political extremists, who were fast leaving the church behind in the political race.

CHRISTIAN LEADERS OF THE NEW AFRICA

Although the leaders of the national struggle have increasingly felt that they have left the church behind, in almost no case have they deserted it. A certain connection, stronger with some men than others, has always been maintained. Most have kept only a nominal Christianity, devoting themselves basically to politics without any thought of the implications of the Christian faith for their actions. In this they are like most of the political leaders of the Western nations. Nkrumah is an example of this type of position; so also are Azikiwe, the president of Nigeria, and Kasavubu and Adoula, the head-of-state and premier respectively of the Congo. Other leaders have a more active relation to the church. Dr. H. Kamuzu Banda, the dominant man of Nyasaland, is an elder in the Presbyterian Church. Joshua Nkomo, the chief African leader of Southern Rhodesia, is a lay preacher in the Methodist Church. Julius Nyerere of Tanganyika is a convinced Roman Catholic, as is Tom Mboya of Kenya. Kenneth Kaunda, who is the principal political leader of Northern Rhodesia, came out of a strongly church-centered training, being the son of a Protestant pastor. Though he has broken with the political conservatism and ineffectivenes that he finds in the church, he still maintains contact with church activities and Christian efforts to help the nation.

A few political leaders not only maintain active contact with the church but also are serious Christians, concerned to bring their faith to bear on their politics. Sir Francis Ibiam, the governor of Eastern Nigeria, and John Karefa-Smart, minister of external affairs for Sierra Leone, are two pre-eminent examples of this type. K. A. Busia, former leader of the opposition in Ghana, and Jason Sendwe, former vice-premier of the Congo, have been two others. Two ordained ministers now fill important political roles: Rev. Ndabingi Sithole is vice-president of the African nationalist organization of Southern Rhodesia and Rev. Richard Andriamanjato is the leader of the chief opposition party in Madagascar and mayor of the island's capital city.

Men of this stripe are, of course, few in Africa, as they are in any part of the world.

A perusal of these names shows at once that the participation of Christians in the national struggle is much greater in the new nations of Africa than in those of Asia. This is because Christians constitute so much larger a part of the population and have taken so much larger a share in general education. Except in the increasingly Muslim countries of West Africa, practically all the educated people of Africa south of the Sahara have come through Christian schools and have at least a nominal Christian background. Even in West Africa it has been noted that of the members of the Ghana legislature elected in 1954, 77 per cent were Christians, and in legislatures of Eastern and Western Nigeria the percentages have been still higher.

Yet despite such close contacts and the nationalist efforts of so many convinced Christians, the church is still regarded by masses of people as an institution of the white man and hence subject to all the resentments created by the white man's rule. The years of domination and exploitation of black by white are not easily to be redeemed.

6

THE PROBLEM OF
A NATIONAL RELIGION

IN JUNE of 1962, a new constitution was promulgated for the Islamic Republic of Pakistan. It declared Pakistan to be a country in which it should be possible for Muslims "to order their lives in accordance with the fundamental principles and basic concepts of Islam and should be provided with facilities whereby they may be enabled to understand the meaning of life according to those principles and concepts."

In these words is set a problem for any Christian. How can a Christian be part of such a country? Christians, along with all minority groups, may be guaranteed the fullest freedom, as they are by this self-same constitution of Pakistan. But can they have freedom to be fully a part of the country or only freedom for living, worshiping, preaching *in* the country? How can a Christian effectively participate in a country whose purpose is to enable Muslims to live in a Muslim way?

GROWING PAINS

Pakistan illustrates most clearly a difficulty that has pressed upon Christians in many of the new nations. When the struggle for national independence filled all the horizon of men's thoughts and actions, the difficulty seldom arose. Men were held together in those days by the opposition to a common enemy, the imperialist power. There was little need of a religious force for unification. But now that independence is achieved, the desire for a unifying religion has increased. The diverse groups of people who made up each new nation tend to pull apart with no common enemy to unite them. A national religion might serve as a unifying force. So the demand grows.

Even where the religious question introduces sharp divisions, as between the Buddhists and Hindus of Ceylon, the call for a national religion is heard. It obviously represents in these cases something deeper than the need for unity. It is part of the search for national identity. The nation-state is an importation. It cannot hope to express the national identity as well as can some traditional element of the people's life. The question, "Who are we Pakistanis or Malays or Burmans or Ceylonese?" can be given an answer with deep appeal if it is said, "We are Muslims or Buddhists or some other religious group." Men have seen the new nation planning its own life and making new laws. They feel the need of some standard by which the desirability of plans and laws can be judged. They are aware that the Western standards are not their own. A national religion might well provide standards with accepted authority behind them.

The hunger for unity and identity gives power to the drive for a national religion and explains why that drive has sometimes been carried on in ways that seem completely foreign to the religion itself. In the discussions of the idea of Pakistan, for example, there were thoughtful believers who said that the tying of Islam to a national ideal would weaken the universal brotherhood of Islam. When Buddhist monks in Ceylon stirred up strife in their campaign for Buddhism, serious Buddhists felt that this contentiousness was a betrayal of Buddhism and constituted a defeat rather than a victory for their religion. But these fears have not caused any widespread concern. The honoring of the traditional religion has provided one way of bringing the old life into the new and of integrating the two, even if some violence is done to each in the process.

Under these circumstances the Christians, who are a minority in all the new nations except some African ones and who do not represent the traditional religion in any, can expect to encounter difficulty as they participate in national life. The extent of the difficulty depends, first, on whether a national religion is officially established and, second, on how far the nation is identified with a particular religion in the popular mind irrespective of its official establishment. In both these regards Christians have found a great variation among the new nations. Sometimes there exists an official religion combined with a popular attitude that excludes people of other religions from full acceptance as members of the nation. Sometimes there is an official religion and yet a far more open attitude among the people. And both kinds of attitude may of course be found where there is no official religion.

THE IDEAL OF AN ISLAMIC SOCIETY

The strongest official and unofficial identification of nation and religion might be expected in the Muslim lands, since Islam has long been known for its extreme social cohesiveness and the exclusion from its community of those who do not profess its faith. Some, but not all, of the Muslim lands do show this pattern. Malaya has made Islam its official religion and provides for the teaching of the faith by government-trained-and-paid teachers in the public schools. In northern Nigeria where the national constitution guarantees religious freedom, there are still reports of discrimination and massive social pressure against non-Muslims. The organization of a political party to represent the Muslim effort to control the government brought forth from the Prime Minister of Western Nigeria a complaint. "It is absolutely intolerable—indeed unthinkable—" said he, "for a group of co-religionists to essay to get themselves into power so that they might lord it over those who do not belong to their faith." [1]

The most obvious example of the Muslim desire for a national religion is, as we have suggested, Pakistan. Pakistan could hardly avoid having an official religion, since it was carved out of the old Indian empire in the belief that the Muslims were a distinct nation and therefore had to have a distinct country of their own. This new country when it came to birth represented the fulfillment of a great dream. Islam, which had shaped a whole civilization in the past, was to become again the formative force in the political and

[1] *Christian Responsibility in an Independent Nigeria*, p. 89. Christian Council of Nigeria, 1961.

social life of a nation. The proper direction of history was to be restored. The Muslim believes that God's rule is made manifest in the historic course of Islam. Something seemed to have gone wrong with this God-sanctioned history in recent centuries as the Muslim world was overrun by the West. Pakistan was to be the restoration of things to their true position. Some believed that the full embodiment of the right society as taught by Islam could be directly established in the constitution and government of the new state.

The years since the birth of Pakistan have been disillusioning and maturing ones. Wilfred Cantwell Smith has pointed out how the great dream failed to provide an adequate inspiration for the people or their leaders. Political intrigue seemed to displace high purpose. The attempt to write an Islamic constitution was subjected to continual frustration. When one was finally drawn up after nine years of effort, it lasted only two years and then revulsion against the politicians led to a military coup and the abrogation of the constitution. Now, following a period of martial law, a new constitution is being tried. Through it all the idea of an Islamic state has prevailed, but agreement on the nature of such a state continues to elude men's grasp.

Commitment to an Islamic state, strangely enough, does not mean that Christians are always barred from joining in the search for the proper form of life for Pakistan. They are not permitted to occupy the highest office of the land nor can they serve as members of the body that has the task of deciding what type of legislation is or is not true to Islam. But they usually have joined with those Muslims who have stood for an interpretation of Islam that would regard all discrimination as un-Islamic and that would give primary attention to the education and advancement of the people as an Islamic duty. As long as this interpretation of Islam prevails, Christians do not need to hesitate in giving their full devotion to the national purposes of an Islamic nation. These are their purposes, too. In Pakistan they are allowed to vote and to hold any but a very few offices, and thus they can, for all practical purposes, take their full part in the nation's life. The problem of a national religion is therefore only a formal problem, if the religion is humanely understood. As long as the state is in practice devoting itself to the service of men, which is also the service to which God calls Christians, the Christians do not have to be greatly concerned about the fact that the state calls itself Islamic. Unfortunately, narrower views of the national purpose and of the nature of Islamic values have at times prevailed. In consequence, Christians have sometimes experienced hostility, discrimination, and intimidation from their fellow citizens of Pakistan.

MILITANT BUDDHISM

Islam is not the only religion that presents such difficulties. The new Buddhist nations of Burma and Ceylon have been as agitated by questions of nation and religion as any Islamic country, despite the reputedly less militant nature of Buddhism. Burma has gone almost as far as Pakistan in establishing an official religion, though, unlike Pakistan, it was not created as a religiously defined nation. Burma, in fact, was inaugurated under frankly secularist leadership, but the trend toward religious establishment set in early and grew steadily. The change was led by the Premier, U Nu, who has guided the affairs of Burma during most of its years of independence and who seems to have undergone quite a change of heart in this respect himself. He has declared that Buddhism offers the strongest basis for Burma's nationhood, and because of this and his own religious convictions he has fostered Buddhism in many ways.

The year 1950 was the decisive one for the change in direction. Starting then, Buddhism was introduced into government schools and higher education, a ministry of religious affairs was established, and the Buddha Sansana, a council of Buddhist organizations, was organized and maintained by the government. Through these means Buddhist missionaries were engaged to go out primarily into the hill country to work among the hill peoples where Christian missions had been pioneering. Every effort was made to turn these people toward Buddhism, endowing monasteries among them and bringing them into Buddhist sacred places. The Karen state, presumably because Karens had so often become Christians, was the only state to be given a ministry of religious affairs, and its concern was only to propagate Buddhism.[2]

Eventually all this led to the establishment of Buddhism as the state religion. That step was taken by a constitutional amendment in 1961. A government commission toured the country beforehand to ascertain the possible reaction of the people, but Christian dissatisfaction was consistently ignored, and it was reported that Christian ministers who were called before the commission were made to feel as if they were on trial. Once the decision was made, the government lost no time in emphasizing through its publicity that to be

[2] Tinker, Hugh. *Union of Burma,* p. 170. New York: Oxford University Press, 1957.

a Burman was to be a Buddhist. So nationality was tied to religion. As events worked out, the state religion was short-lived, for the military revolt in 1962 put an end to the constitution and promptly abolished the provisions for the state religion. The parallel to Pakistan's experience is clear; whether there will be a parallel return to official religion remains to be seen.

THE DESTINY OF LANKA

In Ceylon, as in Burma, the Buddhists entered the era of independence with a longing for government support and direction for their religion. Since the monks and other religious functionaries had no over-all hierarchy of their own, they needed the support and the discipline that the government had exercised in pre-colonial times. Christian missionaries were blamed for the loss of government connections and the loss of labor on temple lands in the era of British rule. Government favoritism was blamed for the disproportionately large number of Christians in official and educational life, an area for which Christians with their long emphasis on schools had been particularly trained.

The government that inaugurated independence in Ceylon was, like its counterpart in Burma, little concerned with those complaints or desires. The year 1956 proved to be the turning point as 1950 was in Burma, but Ceylon's change was far more traumatic. The intellectual preparation for the change came in a large book, *Revolt in the Temple*, by D. C. Vijayavardhana, which held up the vision of "one religion, one race, one language" for the new nation. The emotional preparation came with the publication of *The Betrayal of Buddhism*, the report of a Buddhist Committee of Inquiry set up by the All-Ceylon Buddhist Congress in 1954. This committee declared that Ceylon had been destined to be the stronghold for preserving the purity of Buddhism and attacked Christianity bluntly. "Over Ceylon Christianity sits enthroned and Ceylon bound hand and foot has been delivered at the foot of the cross," [3] was the way they pictured the situation. The particular complaint that lay back of this charge was that the constitution did not give the government sufficient power over the nonreligious activities of religious bodies. The committee believed that the "antinational" work of missionaries should be stopped, that any attempt to convert a person under twenty-one should be a criminal offense, and that no uncompromising religious position, such as that taken by Christianity, should be allowed. "The people of this Buddhist Lanka (Ceylon) are being asked to give it up for crude teaching of unenlightened teachers, for exploded beliefs, outworn theories, and played-out philosophies. The Buddhists do not want to exchange gold for lead or bread for filth," [4] they declared.

The committee secured "general agreement" with their views from one of the major political leaders outside the government. S. W. R. D. Bandaranaike came from a wealthy Christian family but had forsaken his Christianity for Buddhism, whether because he found Buddhism more satisfying, as he said, or because he foresaw the political trends, as some informed observers believed, could hardly be determined. In the election of 1956, Bandaranaike swept into power with the active help of Buddhist monks and the

[3] *The Betrayal of Buddhism, An Abridged Version of the Report of the Buddhist Committee of Inquiry*, p. 31, 1956.
[4] *Ibid.*, pp. iii-iv.

support of the common people, who felt alienated from the Westernized governing group. He inaugurated a period of drastic changes—not drastic enough for the more radical monks, one of whom assassinated him in 1959, but popular enough to ensure the election of his widow as prime minister the year after his death. She continued and intensified his program.

The program was one of providing increasing opportunity and control to the Sinhalese-speaking Buddhist masses of the country. Sinhalese was established as the sole national language at the expense of Tamil, which was spoken by more than 20 per cent of the people, including large numbers of the professional, clerical, and mercantile classes. Civil disobedience followed, with riots and hundreds of killings, the flight of thousands of Tamils from their homes, breakdowns in government, and states of emergency, which kept Ceylon in turmoil.

With the recognition of the Sinhalese language went a recognition of the Buddhist religion. Buddhism was not made the national religion officially, but it was treated in every way as if it were. Government officials celebrated Buddhist occasions and escorted Buddhist relics with great fanfare. The government press was full of publicity for Buddhist activities. Larger numbers of Buddhists were brought into the administration of the country, displacing Christians who had long predominated in this field. The Christian schools, which had formed a major element in the educational system of the country, were presented with impossible conditions to fulfill and then rapidly taken over by the state. Christian administrators of schools were steadily deposed to make way for Buddhists, on the basis of a regulation of 1962 requiring that the head of a school should represent the religion of the majority of the pupils.

The Christian response to these pressures was varied. The Roman Catholics attempted to mount emotional counter-pressures through the encampment of thousands of irate parents in the schools that the government was trying to take over. After some months in which this failed to shake the government's resolution, the schools were relinquished. Protestants tried to keep a few schools by concentrating their resources and attempting to meet the extravagant require-ments of government in a few places, but this proved to be extremely difficult. One group of high officials, largely Christians, planned a *coup d'état* to take over the govern-ment early in 1962, but they were arrested before this could take place. The Governor General, also a Christian, re-signed following the arrests.

The leadership of the Protestant churches, however, tried to take a very different line in response, refraining from counterpressures and attempting to hold up a larger vision of what the Christian contribution should be in a pre-dominantly Buddhist nation. They saw the Christian role as that of servant and reconciler. They recognized the legiti-macy of many of the Buddhist complaints. It had been true that under the British rule, Christians, as the group most eager to develop education, had had an advantage over other groups and Buddhism had not received the protection and care that, lacking internal organization, it needed. They stressed that the church should be more concerned with its life and mission than with the protection of itself as an institution. And they suggested to the nation that a common national culture might develop from diverse sources, Christian as well as Buddhist, for any culture grows through the influence of many forces upon it.[5] In these ways the Christians of Ceylon, like those of Pakistan, hoped to take a responsible part in the life of the nation even though they did not share the national religion.

THE SECULAR STATE

This is not to suggest that the Pakistani and Ceylonese situations were the most desirable ones in Christian eyes. That which is desirable is by now fairly clear. The Christians of the new nations, or at least the Protestants among them, have done sufficient thinking together to reach a large measure of agreement as to what they want to see in the relations between nation and religion. A whole series of conferences of Asian Christians and at least one of Asians and Africans together have consistently come to the same conclusion when they take up the question of religion and the state. The conclusion is summed up in the phrase "the secular state." This is the state that gives no support to any religion and makes no restriction on any beyond the minimal requirements of public order and morality. It is not anti-religious, but it eschews any identification of itself with the divine or the absolute. It knows that it is limited to this age, or *saeculum* (hence the name), and that it has no business determining the ultimate loyalties of men. It recognizes that religious faith represents an area in the lives of persons that is beyond its competence and over which it dare not lay any claim.

[5] See the report of the conference of Protestant leaders held at Uduvil Girls' College in 1961, *Christian Witness in Contemporary Ceylon*. Jaffna, Ceylon: St. Joseph's Catholic Press, 1961.

The goals of such a state are determined by the very fact that it recognizes that men have an ultimate loyalty and a point of reference that lie beyond its control. Men are thereby seen to possess a dignity that lifts them above the state. It must be the state's goal, then, to serve men, creating the conditions of physical welfare, liberty, justice, and a community of mutual concern that will enable them to develop fully as human beings.

This view of the state's obligation to men is implicit in such internationally recognized documents as the Universal Declaration of Human Rights and the Declaration of Principles of UNESCO. In the UNESCO declaration we read of "dignity, equality, and respect for the human person" as providing the standard for social life. Therefore, it is not a view of the state that is limited to persons of the Christian faith but one that has a wide acceptance throughout the entire world.

Christians who hold this view of what the state should be would, of course, be just as much opposed to the nation identifying itself with Christianity or the Christian God as they would be to any other religious identification. The Protestants of the Philippines, for example, objected vigorously when in 1956 the government of their country decided to consecrate the nation to the Sacred Heart of Jesus. This was not only an objection to the Roman Catholic phraseology of the action but to the action itself, as being beyond the proper sphere of affairs of the state. Such Christians, in the Philippines or in any other country, would likewise oppose any discrimination against non-Christians such as the persecution of Buddhists that has been reported from South Viet Nam.

AGAINST THE STREAM

But though the secular state has so thoroughly established itself as the choice of Protestant Christians in Asia and Africa, it must be admitted that it is not an arrangement that is congenial to the traditional life of those continents. Only in the last two or three centuries has it begun to be accepted in Western life and thought. In Asia and Africa the permeation of all social and cultural life by a single religious outlook has continued to be the prevailing pattern. In such a situation it is much more difficult to create a truly secular state than in those areas where secularity has been widely accepted in many segments of life. Even in the United States it is only now being realized how far practice has failed to follow the principle of a secular state as enunciated in its Constitution, because the social and cultural life had been so saturated with religious practices and perspectives.

In Asia and Africa there is an additional difficulty. As we have seen, the traditional religions do not have anything that corresponds to the church as an organized body enrolling all believers yet distinct from the state or from society as a whole. Therefore the religious institutions are not well equipped to survive under a secular state, and there is consequent constant pressure against the secular ideal. In some cases religious groups may recoil from a secular structure for the nation because their adherents have not been accustomed to seeing themselves in such a way that their individual identity can be distinguished from the cultural group as a whole. Where tribal religions have prevailed, they have given the individual no ultimate standing ground except as a part of his tribe. Even the great mystical religions of the Orient, while they see the essence of each man as something that rises above and passes through many earthly relationships and individualities, do not usually grant the person in his present individuality with his own unique characteristics any place to stand except as a part of his cultural group. Islam recognizes, with Christianity, an ultimate standpoint and an eternal destiny for each individual, but with the strong sense of group solidarity that prevails among Muslims there has been little readiness to find in this a reason for seeing the individual Muslim apart from his society. Thus it is much harder for these religions to accept individual religious freedom or a national structure in which religion is not overtly tied to the life of the nation. Under these circumstances the establishment and implementation of the secular state is sure to be a difficult process.

PRACTICAL PROBLEMS

These theoretical difficulties become very concrete when we look at the countries where a secular state has been tried. India is the shining example of such a country, but India also reveals what enormous obstacles exist to the acceptance of the secular idea. We have already seen how church and mission have been under attack in independent India for being "anti-national." This kind of attack may be due to some actual isolation of Christians from national life and problems, but it may also be due to an unexpressed assumption that only Hindus are true nationals of India. The cry of right-wing agitators, "Hindi, Hindu, Hindustan," making a complete identity of language, religion, and nationality, gives this assumption frighteningly clear expression. There are prominent Indian industrialists who have agitated for a constitutional amendment making India a theocratic state with the president a "Defender of the Faith" like the Queen of England, and in one of the smaller states, Manipur, Christians have been ordered along with others to observe certain days for the propitiation of gods and demons.

More subtle and therefore more difficult to resist have been the attempts on the part of the Congress party and of the state and national governments in India to foster spiritual and moral values and thereby to become the enforcers, often unwittingly, of Hindu types of belief. The attempt to develop "common worship" of a syncretistic type in the public schools of the country, for example, has caused great concern among Christians. They find in it an essentially Hindu approach to religious life, leaving no place for the recognition of the fact that there may be crucial issues of religious truth on which each person must make a decision.

Indonesia is another country that Christians regard as maintaining more or less a secular state. But Indonesia shows not only, like India, the difficulty of putting the idea into practice but also the difficulty of keeping the idea itself clear. The arrangement there is that no single religion is officially favored, but the state gives assistance and support to all religions. One might, therefore, say that although no particular religion is established, religion in general is established. The constitution says that "the state shall be based upon belief in the God of all mankind," and guarantees freedom for men in their particular religions. The Indonesian nation in its foundation was said to be grounded on the Pantjasila or five principles—nationalism, humanity, representative government, social justice, and belief in God.

This was regarded as summing up the nature of Indonesian nationality, and clearly belief in God was considered indispensable. A more recent formulation of the national ideology that has been officially advocated is called Nasagkom, a word that is composed of the first syllables of the words for nationalism, religion, and communism. In all of these statements it is made very evident that the state is tied to religion.

Yet Christians have in general been ready to accept this as an alternative form of the secular state, since it treats all religions equally, helping all rather than remaining separate from all. In point of fact, this means very little help for Christianity, since it counts only 5 per cent of the people, and very considerable help for Islam. The appeal that this has for Christians is that it gives them as a religious group a recognized place in the life of the state, and doubtless it serves to take some of the edge off the ever present Muslim demand for an Islamic state. Also the powerful emotions of nationalism no doubt do their part to still any critical thoughts that may arise about an ideology that so clearly links religion and nationalism as do Nasagkom and the Pantjasila.

Only when pressure for the official ideology is brought to bear directly on the church do doubts begin to appear. For instance, in the spring of 1962, all Christian schools received an inquiry from the government as to what they were prepared to do to foster the approved ideology for the realization of the national aspirations. Here it begins to become apparent that what is present in essence is not so much the establishment of religion in general as the establishment of an artificially created national religion.

THE GREAT CONFIDENCE GAME

At this point we glimpse a further difficulty of the secular state, one that is far more evident in certain other countries than it is in Indonesia. This is the tendency of a secular state to rush into the area of man's ultimate loyalties that it has vacated for the sake of its secular character and which, therefore, has for it something of the pull of a vacuum. Since there is no recognized religion to fill this area of the common life, there develops a widespread desire to fill it with a pseudo-religion created by the state or by the people of the nation. The Communist countries offer the most blatant examples of this. More moderate expressions of it can be found in most of the secular states of the Western world. Will Herberg's book, *Protestant, Catholic, Jew,* shows how far the "American way of life" has become the operative faith for the American people, the faith for which men are unashamedly intolerant, the faith that has its own compulsory rituals to compensate for the prohibited public performance of traditional religious rites, the faith that allows for no higher standards from which it can be criticized. In the new nations, with their still divided populations, there is an even greater pull toward the establishment of such pseudo-religions when there is no recognized religion to unify the people.

The substitute faith may be promoted in far more obvious ways in the new nations than in the West. Kwame Nkrumah has allowed the creation of a religious cult around his own person that openly proclaims him the redeemer. "He is our Messiah and he is immortal," declares one of Ghana's leading newspapers. The Anglican bishop of Accra was expelled from the country for a time because he dared to criticize the religious beliefs the government's youth movement was inculcating in children. In Nyasaland the ruling party has officially declared that the titles of Messiah and Savior shall be used exclusively for Dr. H. Kamuzu Banda, the prime minister who is also an officer of the church. The young Nigerian Christian, Edmund Ilogu, has warned of the danger of a nationalist religion being developed in his country. If Christianity does not serve as the spiritual fountainhead for nationalist commitment and thought and thus keep nationalism healthy, he says, then nationalism will create its own spiritual sources and religious expressions that will be very unhealthy.

THE BURDEN OF DISENCHANTMENT

The church's great task in the secular state, then, is to keep the state truly secular. It does this best by giving to men an understanding of why the state should be secular, why it serves its purpose most truly if it neither makes a god of itself nor explicitly identifies itself with the teachings of religion. This will not be an easy task for the church. It will seem like an odd thing for the church to call men to the kind of nationhood where the ultimate religious foundations and religious loyalties are never recognized by the community as a whole. It would seem much more congenial for the church to call upon the nation to recognize the ultimate grounds and goals on which and for which it stands. But that condition cannot exist without some element of compulsion denying man's ultimate dignity and freedom and the reduction of some people to second-class citizenship. In the age in which we live, if men are to have freedom in questions of religious belief and hold their beliefs voluntarily, then we can be sure that they will not all recognize the same religious loyalty. In this age it is a choice between an enforced, unwilling uniformity, which can only be repulsive to those who recognize the dignity of man made in the image of God, and a secular state, which allows for variety in these matters. The choice for a secular state means, to be sure, that the area of national action, an ever growing area of modern life, will have to be kept devoid of any recognition of the ultimate foundations on which it stands and the ultimate purposes that it serves, and this is not an attractive prospect. It will mean an ever growing area for the studied avoidance of ultimate questions, as if such questions did not exist. But the answer to such difficulties is not a reversion to involuntary, external religious unity, but rather the wider dissemination by the church through all society of the voluntary acknowledgment of the God who is Lord of the nations.

Were the time ever to come when God's rule was freely recognized and God's purpose freely acknowledged by the whole people, then the nation in its voluntary structures would be in a position to acknowledge its service to God. But even then it would as an element of that service keep the official and coercive powers of the state on a secular level, devoid of any religious expression, in order to allow men full freedom to differ from the general consensus. Man's relationship to God would continue to be the point at which man would be seen as a free being because he is related to that which is beyond the social structure and social controls. And if this secular type of state ought to be maintained, even in a religiously united nation, how much more necessary it is that it be maintained in the actual situations of religious variety that are to be found in all the new nations of the world.

Nor should this be limited to the new nations. The logic of the secular state applies just as strongly to every nation where man's freedom and dignity under God is to be recognized. In fact, if the Christian plea for a secular state is going to carry any force in the new nations where the Christians are a minority, then it must be equally pressed in old nations where Christians are a majority. Christians have no right to expect a freedom in the one case that they deny in the other. The case for a secular state in Asia or Africa depends to no small extent on how ready Christians are to support the same outlook in Europe or North America.

7

THE CHURCH SERVING
THE NATION

THE common man in the new nations today is like a stick of dynamite planted in the midst of the world. He appears harmless enough, but he may blow up at any time, bringing the world's structure down in ruins around him. He is as a rule a villager following his traditional life and holding on to the tribal or family ties that have always brought him security. His pace is slow and leisurely, untouched by the pressures of modern existence. Yet he is fully accustomed to hard work from morning to night, to malnutrition and sickness and early death. He is mired in poverty and debt from which none of his forefathers ever thought of escaping. He is illiterate, which means he is cut off from the communication with the wider world that reading brings.

At the same time, he is excited by new ideas and new sights. He sees that the village headman now owns a tractor with which he cultivates the fields alongside the men who still use the wooden plows and short-handled hoes. The political party representatives with flags flying and drums beating come to the village from time to time to make fiery speeches and to promise bright futures. He hears of five-year plans and international assistance programs. He has a sense of political power within his reach now that the colonial rulers have left, though this power does not seem to have made him better off. The village has more children growing up in it, and it is harder for people to find employment. The young people in increasing numbers go off to the city to look for work, hoping there to make a better living, to escape the drudgery of labor on the land, and to enjoy the bright lights and excitement of urban existence. But there, too, they find unemployment or underemployment facing them. A few tips for keeping a watch on parked cars may be all they can get to live on, and they soon lose all the traditional morality they brought with them. They have high hopes and deep discontents and are ready for any excitement that comes along.

It is the situation of these people that makes the life of the new nations such a precarious one today. Independence has come. With freedom, everyone holds high hopes of a better life. But agricultural techniques remain backward, industry is still in its infancy, and old loyalties still divide the people. Their hopes, therefore, cannot be quickly fulfilled, and their excessive expectations may lead them into frustration and disillusionment. To make matters worse, the population explosion proceeds apace, so that whatever advances are achieved tend to be swallowed up by the additional mouths to be fed. The prospects are omi-

nous unless every nerve is strained to pull the nations out
of the straits they are in. Many leaders of the new nations
recognize the gravity of the problem they face and are
trying to stir their people to an effort greater than that
they made in the struggle for independence. But it is
more difficult to galvanize whole populations to fight poverty, divisiveness, illiteracy, and backwardness than it was
to fight a foreign ruler. The new struggle involves breaking
with attitudes and traditions that have been accepted and
appreciated as the colonial powers never were. Further-
more, the new struggle calls for resources in technical
training and financing that the old struggle never required.

The world as a whole needs to be awake to the new
struggle. The nations in which it is going on cover most
of the world's two largest continents. That great a portion
of the earth's surface and its population cannot be in danger without the whole world being in danger. The situation is far more critical than when colonialism was the
big issue. The new problems are more complex and difficult to overcome than was colonial rule. And if they are
not overcome, the consequences for the world in terms of
widespread confusion and economic collapse will be far
more destructive.

"YOUR SERVANTS FOR JESUS' SAKE"

Something of great significance has been going on in
the churches of the new nations during these early years
of national independence. As their homelands have struggled to cope with the massive problems that confront them,
the churches have been stirred by a deeper sense of

identification with their nations and a desire to help in the solution of those problems. Whatever they may think about any national religion or whatever their stance may have been during the independence struggle, they know now that their task is to help meet the needs of their country. They see themselves as one with their fellow citizens, sharing with them in whatever successes and suffering with them in whatever failures their nation meets.

The churches in their organized form can provide only a limited amount of service. Larger contributions are possible through the work of their members in daily occupations. Christian teachers, doctors, politicians, mechanics, and laborers can extend the field of service to the nation far beyond what the organized church is able to do. Therefore, the emphasis is more and more on the "lay apostolate," seeing the individual gifts of the lay members that are used for the upbuilding of the nation as a service rendered by the church. The whole body of Christian men and women, as the body of Christ in a particular nation, are called upon to throw themselves into the life of that nation, to serve that nation in its political, economic, educational, and ethical needs and to bind the citizenry together in a sense of brotherhood and mutual responsibility.

Evidence that the churches are thinking seriously in terms of this new orientation comes from country after country. From India comes a book on *Christian Participation in Nation Building.* Ceylon produces a report on *Christian Witness in Contemporary Ceylon.* Nigerian Christians have published a booklet on *Christian Responsibility in an Independent Nigeria* and those of Ghana have made a statement on *The Role of the Christian Church in a Demo-*

cratic State. All are in agreement with the Indian document which says that "the social responsibility of the church at the present time is to participate in the ongoing movements of national development."[1] Burman Christians have said that there is now "a more public Christian participation in the national undertaking than ever before."[2] The whole program of Christian service as it has been developed in the past is being called up for reconsideration and recasting in light of the national needs. Christian service must not be seen as an isolated phenomenon but must be set against the total program of national development, trimmed at one place and extended at another in order to make the greatest possible contribution to the program. In lands as far apart as Korea and Nigeria studies have appeared documenting the contribution of Christian service to the over-all national effort.

We should not suppose that all Christians in the new nations have embraced the new outlook expressed in these reports and studies. These show only the direction of thought among the leaders and the more articulate members of the churches. At the local level in the village church often as not the members have seen nothing of the vision of national needs beyond the immediate problems that they themselves feel. They are undernourished and underemployed, and they must bend every effort to maintain their

[1] Devanandan, P. D., and Thomas, M. M. *Christian Participation in Nation Building,* p. 209. Bangalore: National Christian Council of India, 1960.

[2] Eastern Asia Christian Conference, Bangkok, 1949. *The Christian Prospect in Eastern Asia,* p. 11. New York: published for International Missionary Council and World Council of Churches by Friendship Press, 1949.

own existence. But in this they are a typical part of the nation, and theirs are the very problems with which the nation must be dealing. As they work on their own needs, they are working on the nation's. Thus any tendency to isolation and a ghetto-like existence in the local life of the church is partly counteracted by the very needs that it meets in its isolation.

The greater identification with the nation has meant for most Christians a greater openness toward their fellow nationals of other faiths. The Christians are too small a group in most of the new nations to make much of an impact on the enormous needs around them if they try to work alone. They must work with men of other religious groups. So conferences and discussion programs have sprung up between Christians and others, as they try to see how their paths converge in the nation's service even though they begin from different religious starting points. The Christian Institute for the Study of Religion and Society, which has been established in South India, has sponsored a number of symposia and joint publications in which Christians and others have discussed the great issues before the nation. In this way common grounds and common goals are hammered out. The cooperative efforts are not to be seen, in the present thinking of the church, as a way of bringing any pressure on other people to become Christians. The integrity of the common task must be held too high to allow for that. In some places young Christian leaders are saying that all religious labels should be laid aside when Christians enter the field of service, because they find that any attempt to give their service the label of "Christian" is suspect, in light of past misuse,

as being a form of aggressiveness or a bait for evangelization.

It would be idle to deny that there are dangers in this
new outlook. The attempt to find a common basis for
service that is acceptable to all may weaken the open acknowledgment of the deeper Christian bases. The strong
public demand for help in national advancement and the
general public antipathy to any form of preaching may
produce a one-sided Christian witness where the stress is
on those activities that will avoid offense and bring popularity, to the neglect of those things that are likely to
bring difficulty. In these situations, as in all others, the
church must remember that it does not serve the nation
because the nation is its master but because its true Master
calls it to serve its neighbors.

There are four fields of service to which the church
finds itself particularly called in the new nations today;
they mark the four areas of most urgent national need. The
first is the need for national unity; the second, the need
for education; the third, the need for democracy; and the
fourth, the need for economic development. Each of these
requires thoughtful attention if the church's service is to
be given appropriately and effectively.

NATIONAL UNITY

Inevitably national unity must come first, because without it there can be no nation and no concerted grappling
with the other needs that face it. Nearly all the new nations
face serious ethnic, religious, or linguistic divisions harking
back to the pre-national days when men found their community in kinship, in tribal, language, or religious groups.

These can threaten the very existence of the nation. Paul Devanandan, describing this post-independence experience, has declared: "We are now free to determine our own political destiny. . . . Today our main concern is to work for and achieve a real sense of national solidarity." [3]

The expected thing might be for Christians to take their place as one more division in the nation, in this case a religious one. Often in the smaller circles of village life they have fallen into this position, just as in Western lands the various churches in a city or town have often added to the forces of division rather than seeing their task as a unifying one for the whole community. A report from India at the time of independence tells how after a village church service held among the poorest and most oppressed people "a number of Christian villagers gathered . . . and asked with some feeling, 'How long must we go on serving others without demanding any rights for ourselves?' " and goes on to comment on the existence of "a growing spirit of communalism which is noisily expressing itself in demands for separate political representation and safeguards for the Christian community." [4] Christians from the West who in their divisiveness have had far less need to protect themselves from others can well understand how a body of Christians may act in this way.

But where Christians have been awakened to their calling, whether in East or in West, they have tried to bring men together in working for the common welfare rather than separating themselves off as a special interest group.

[3] Devanandan, P. D. *The Gospel and Renascent Hinduism*, p. 24. London: S.C.M. Press, 1959.
[4] *National Christian Council Review*, LXVII (1947), p. 630.

Those who preach a gospel of reconciliation have had to recognize that their message commits them to working for reconciliation on the level of national life. So Christians in India have struggled against caste divisions and against the religious communalism, which has caused such problems for Indian political life. They have been active in the recent "national integration" effort launched to combat the divisiveness stemming from newly established linguistic states and newly revived Hindu and Muslim political parties. In Ceylon Christians have tried to emphasize all that the Sinhalese and Tamil people have in common and have declared that everywhere "the ideal of a united Ceylonese nation should be unrelentingly held up." [5] In the time of troubles that descended upon Ceylon with the attempt to force unity on a Sinhalese basis, they have called for a strong national government committed to integration and development, which runs against Tamil demands, and yet with elected councils holding subordinate authority for distinct language areas, which is counter to Sinhalese desires. Though Christians have been backward in their use of Sinhalese, the new united theological college begun in 1963 is claimed to be the first college in the country to teach in the national language.

DIVISIONS IN AFRICA

In Africa Christian bodies have tried to work for national unity where they are living with other strong religious groups. Efforts have been made in Ghana, Nigeria, and Cameroun, where there are large Muslim as well as

[5] *Christian Witness in Contemporary Ceylon*, p. 52. Jaffna, Ceylon: St. Joseph's Catholic Press, 1961.

Christian elements in the population, to bring the two groups into cooperation. The Christian Council of Nigeria has sponsored a statement advocating a strong federal government even though this will doubtless mean the domination of the smaller Christian South by the great Muslim North. The church in Africa has also been a force for breaking down the tribal divisions, which are the greatest threat to the unity of the African states. Occasionally churches in earlier days were established on tribal lines, and in those cases the continued life of the church serves to perpetuate tribal consciousness within the national life. But for the most part churches have not been limited to one tribe, so their principal effect has been to bridge the divisions rather than to maintain them. Where there are evidences of a revival of tribalism today, as in southern Congo, the church is proving to be a considerable bridging force. And everywhere the constant teaching of the church that moral obligations transcend the tribal communities and apply equally to all men has had a weakening effect upon the separate compartments into which the nations of Africa were formerly divided. An old chief in Ghana, watching one day as the pupils of a Christian boarding school, drawn from many different tribal groups over a wide area of the country, paraded past their school building, shook his head in wonder. He remarked that when he was a boy it would have been unthinkable for children from any of those alien groups to have set foot on the soil where that school was built. Such was the unifying effect of the church.

We cannot speak of these positive stands for unity without recognizing the other side in Africa, the weakness of the church in overcoming racial divisions in its own life and in the population at large and the negative impact on the nation of Christian denominational divisions, especially through the activity of the noncooperating missions, which are so important in Africa. For recognized leaders in the African church, such as John and Rena Karefa-Smart of Sierra Leone, Christianity has played so much more the divisive than the unifying role in its racial and denominational divisions that in their book, *The Halting Kingdom,* they present this as one of the two or three important failures of Christianity on that continent. Yet for them, as for all the leaders of the churches in the new nations, the recognition of a failure carries with it an acknowledgment of the true reality of the church's life. The church is not another division within the life of the nation but a body of men set free by Christ, free from self-regarding worries and the desire for recognition, free to serve the nation and to bind its people together in brotherly love.

SERVING IN EDUCATION

Education, like unity, is basic for the development of a new nation. Only as the people receive education will they have the information that will enable them to be responsible citizens and the concern that will lead them to work for economic development. Without education they remain as they have been in the past, unable to help their nation as it tries to make its way in the modern world, uninterested in new methods, unable to use effectively the resources for economic advance. Those who study the process of national development declare that education is the first step in that process. Therefore Paul Devanandan's statement about unification as the main task following independence must be balanced by an African Christian declaration on the primacy of education for independence: "The rallying cry of 'self-government now' has been superseded by that of 'education now.' " [6]

To be a new nation, then, is to be a nation obsessed with education. Nigeria is putting 40 per cent of its national budget into education. Malaya in the ten years leading up to independence increased its budget for education tenfold. Indonesia raised its literacy rate from 10 per cent at the time of independence to 50 per cent a decade later. In its first decade as a nation, Ceylon doubled its educational system. India tripled its colleges in its first decade and a half. The African nations at a conference held at Addis Ababa in May, 1961, adopted a twenty-year plan that had as the objectives to be achieved at completion universal primary education, 30 per cent of high-school age youths in school, and 20 per cent of college age young people in colleges.

The churches are ready to integrate their educational efforts into these national plans. The African churches held a meeting in Salisbury at the end of 1962 as a followup of the Addis Ababa Conference to discuss their contribution to the future of African education. The dominant tone of their meeting was one of eagerness to help in the task ahead. The African nations were seen to be undertaking a huge burden, and it was felt that the churches should help shoulder it as much as possible. Certainly it was recognized that the governments will increasingly de-

[6] Matthews, Z. K. "Christian Education in a Changing Africa," *International Review of Missions,* LII (January 1963), p. 38.

velop schools of their own in preference to making further grants to church schools. But this is no reason for the churches to lessen their contribution where it is still badly needed. This attitude, which was dominant at Salisbury, is fairly typical of the outlook of the churches in all the new nations. Most of the governments, in their turn, are happy to have the Christian contribution maintained.

In some countries the effect of new government policies will be to make life difficult for the church schools. In Ceylon, Christian schools have been largely forced out of existence. In Burma, too, the government cut off help to church schools, though the schools were not faced with impossible conditions for continuation as they were in Ceylon. Most of them have continued to give valuable service by maintaining high standards of education. The Burman government also seized, with some compensation, the major Christian College, Judson College, and also the buildings erected by the church with government approval to provide a replacement for Judson. In Pakistan the government has ordered all Christian schools to teach the doctrines of Islam to Muslim pupils and has forbidden Bible study for any who are not Christians. Where such restrictions are imposed, the churches can give their help only in the more limited form that is allowed under government policies.

A further way lies open for service to education even when there are no Christian schools. Christian teachers can make their contribution to national education through work in the government schools and through the attempt to grapple from a Christian perspective with all of the problems arising in them. This kind of service is increasingly emphasized in the churches today, and it will doubt-less grow in emphasis as the demand for government teachers increases.

Christians, whether in government or church schools, are concerned that human values be maintained in education. Strong pressures are now appearing to treat education only in terms of its national values. The Addis Ababa Conference spoke of educational development as a highly profitable form of investment, which would pay good returns in the economic life of a country. Advisers to the new governments have been telling them that students must be required to take those courses that will advance national development rather than those courses that might be of most value to them personally. Christians must surely demonstrate a large degree of understanding for these emphases in the present precarious situation of the new nations. Increased study of those subjects that will be most valuable for the nation's development is assuredly called for when the nation's viability is hanging in the balance. But while this emphasis is being made, the individual student and his needs for a fuller life should not be lost to sight. Teachers who will care about the individual student and his growth as a whole person are particularly needed in a system that has to emphasize national values.

DIFFICULTIES OF DEMOCRACY

Democracy, that magic word of modern politics that every nation applies to its own system of government but that each defines in its own way, has had a complicated career in the new nations. When the movement toward national independence was in full swing, it involved larger and larger elements of the population in political activity and hence, in one sense, the move was toward greater democracy. In that sense the life of the new nations has continued in a fairly consistent democratic direction because the programs and policies of their governments have induced larger numbers of the people to participate in national affairs.

But the prospects for democracy in the sense of really responsible participation by the people through free elections and a dual- or multi-party system have never been bright. Their dimness is due to the low level of literacy, the lack of a sense of individual responsibility in the traditional societies, and the shortage of national leaders with political experience. These factors have made it easy for the machinery of democracy, where it was bequeathed to the new nations by the departing European powers, to be taken over by an autocrat or by corrupt politicians who give the people no opportunity to participate in national affairs except as a massive rubber stamp for their own will. Besides, there are always lurking in the wings of the stage the army officers, men who represent Western efficiency and up-to-date methods in their training and who may seize the leading role if the elected rulers prove lacking in vigor. So democracy follows an uncertain course in these nations. In four of them—Sudan, Pakistan, Burma, and Korea— military dictatorships have been created and in others of them a one-man rule has gradually been put into effect.

Even when there is no obvious dictatorship there is a strong tendency toward a one-party state. Sometimes the one-party system is officially established. At other times a multiplicity of parties is allowed, but in fact one party completely dominates political life. This is most obvious in the new African states. In Ghana the Convention Peoples party won nearly 90 per cent of the votes in 1960. In Nyasaland the Malawi Congress got 99 per cent of the votes. The same percentage went to the Democratic party in the Ivory Coast. TANU captured 70 out of 71 seats in the Tanganyika legislature, and the Progressive party won 80 out of 81 seats in Senegal. In the Asian states when elections have been held the figures have not been so extreme, but none of them has developed an opposition party that can mount a serious threat to the government. In some countries, as in India, the opposition parties are extremely vocal and have made a considerable impact upon government policy, but in none of the new nations except the Philippines, Jordan, and Lebanon has there been an actual transfer of power from one party to another as a result of a national election.

There are understandable reasons for one-party dominance. In the fight for freedom party disputes could have been disastrous for the national cause, so one party represented the nation, and it has continued to do so after independence. In the uncertainties that surround the life of a new nation in the world, it is still felt that all must pull together to save the national cause and therefore opposition parties are regarded as a luxury. Where, as in Africa, there is the possibility of parties lining up with tribes or ethnic divisions, the introduction of more than one party could still bring disaster for the nation. Hence it may be a long time before dual- or multi-party systems can be expected to develop or even should be desired in the new nations. In the meantime, as Julius Nyerere of Tanganyika has said, it is more important to emphasize safeguards for the rights of the individual as the touchstone of democracy in these lands. Freedom of speech and belief, freedom from arbitrary arrest, and the right to a fair trial are more basic to democracy than a two-party political structure, and the more basic things should be given attention first.

IN SERVICE OF DEMOCRACY

Every element of democracy requires constant attention and vigorous support from the citizenry if it is to survive. In this fact lies a challenge to the churches. They are usually too small to have any great effect on the political system. But they can, where allowed, add their voices to those raised in support of democracy. This they have fairly consistently done. At a conference of Asian Christian leaders in Sumatra in 1957 there was complete agreement expressed "that democratic polity comes closest to the fulfilment of the Christian ideal of man's organized life," [7] and the reasons for this conclusion were carefully detailed. The Indonesian Council of Churches in 1960, as one-man rule was strengthening its grip on their country, declared bravely that citizens should have the right to supervise the exercise of power by their rulers. In Ghana the Christian Council, also in 1960 when many people in other parts of the world feared that that country was losing its democracy, spoke of its assurance that the nation would not abolish freedom of criticism. It extolled democracy, with

[7] Asian Christian Study Conference, Pematang Siantar. *The Social Goals of the New Asia*, p. 13. Geneva: World Council of Churches, 1957.

freedom of action for voluntary organizations, as the best social and political system. At other times, Ghana's Christian leaders have pleaded for the rights of those imprisoned without trial. In Nigeria, the Christian Council has opposed the idea of a one-party state. Indian Christians have issued a book titled *India's Quest for Democracy* and have urged that the church provide for its members a sustained program of education for democracy. Even in Korea, though the undemocratic Rhee government was led by Christians and influential Christians gave it uncritical support, there was some expression of concern by the National Christian Council for the preservation of democratic freedom, and a mass meeting of Christians was held in a "save the nation" appeal "to secure democratic stability and safeguard human rights." [8] However, these protestations by Korean Christians came early in the Rhee regime, and it was not till after the overthrow of that regime that Christians began any serious heart-searching as to their responsibilities for democracy and the need of a critical attitude toward even an independent Korean government.

The most fundamental contribution that the church can make to democracy is to be true to its own nature. It must preach and act its own deep belief in the value of every man as he is seen in relation to God. When it does so, it will challenge all undemocratic ways of treating persons. The traditional social structures in the new nations are ridden with authoritarian standards and relationships. The joint-family system, the caste system, the tribal organiza-

[8] Eastern Asia Christian Conference, Bangkok, 1949. *The Christian Prospect in Eastern Asia,* p. 4. New York: Published for International Missionary Council and World Council of Churches by Friendship Press, 1949.

tion, and the village community all have their authoritarian qualities. They hang, as one Asian leader put it, as "halters around our neck" in the march toward freedom and justice. The structures are not necessarily to be abandoned, for they have much of enduring value in them. But they must be infused with a new spirit. The church, which believes in and proclaims God's love for each individual, can be a source of that new spirit.

SERVING FOR ECONOMIC DEVELOPMENT

Finally we must come to that need of the new nations that most people think of first, the need for economic development. The new nations are also the poor nations. Without economic advances their people sink into ever deeper poverty as the population grows. The result is that the national life becomes more unstable and more susceptible to the extremes of communism and fascism. The amount that the churches can do to bring about economic progress, like political progress, is limited because of their limited size. But the inability to do great things is no excuse for failing to do small ones, and some of the small ones can be significant.

Economists agree that the most important ingredients for economic advance are not themselves economic. Enthusiasm, determination, a sense of the importance of the work to be done are prerequisites for the vigorous effort that is required in the economic development of nations. Many important advances in economic productivity can be made with very little technical knowledge or financial resources if only these qualities of the spirit are in good supply. The assurance of social justice in the use of the goods produced is equally important in securing the willingness of men to work. Few people will put much effort into economic advances that are for the benefit of only the wealthy.

In these fields the churches see contributions that they can make. They believe that one of the best kinds of help they can give to their country is to spread the Christian belief in the dignity of labor, including manual labor, which is so often despised. They can also inculcate the sense of divine vocation in daily work, which will lead men to put their best efforts into their tasks and to do them with honesty. Christians can also manifest their concern for social justice. Paul Abrecht has shown in his book, *The Churches and Rapid Social Change,* that it was Christian missions that served as the pioneers in urban social work among the victims of injustice in Asia and Africa. Missions also inaugurated a notable program of peasant cooperatives and other forms of agricultural service, in size smaller only than the educational and medical services they provided. These programs normally need to be continued as a supplement to what the new governments can do. Yet, as Abrecht also points out, this kind of social service needs to be set in the context of a concern for social justice. "Today," he writes, "social change has to be seen primarily in terms of social justice, because it requires the search for new social structures and the development of social welfare on a national rather than an individual or tribal basis." [9] The consistent advocacy of land reform that the Asian churches have shown in their conferences during the past decade, the series of studies of social problems coming out of Asian

[9] Abrecht, Paul. *The Churches and Rapid Social Change,* p. 200. New York: Doubleday and Co., Inc., 1961.

and African churches, and the beginning of Asian meetings on industrial evangelism aimed at understanding the needs of industrial workers are evidence of a growing interest among Christians in the problems of social justice.

More direct economic contributions are also within the capacity of the churches. The inauguration of a new government may well be accompanied by dislocations and confusion that leaves masses without food or work. The churches can help with relief programs. At the time of the division of India and Pakistan, church relief efforts played a significant role in caring for the millions of refugees. More recently in that area, the churches have launched their largest and most long-term program of relief and rehabilitation, the Bengal Refugee Service, designed to establish new villages and small industries for the refugees in Bengal. Likewise, in Israel, the churches have carried on a seemingly endless task of caring for displaced persons. In the Congo, a large program of relief was launched when normal government and economic life broke down. Most recently the churches have organized on an international basis the Christian Committee for Service in Algeria, providing work in a reforestation program for twelve thousand people and food for seventy-two thousand during the period of economic displacement that has followed hard on independence.

Relief work is often connected with technical training and services as a type of rehabilitation. In the Congo crisis, American churches saw the need for more than immediate relief donations and proceeded to set up, through a special foundation cooperating with other interested groups, the Congo Polytechnic Institute. Within two years, over a hundred qualified teachers and technicians were sent to the Congo to work with this institute. Pre-university, agriculture, and home economics courses have been started, and plans drawn for the provision of further types of technical training, such as public health, engineering, and mechanics. This is only one example of the many technical training projects that the churches have maintained in Asia and Africa over the years. There have been industrial schools, agricultural colleges, industrial testing laboratories, technical service programs, capital funds for village industries, seed and fertilizer experiments, and other projects that are making a contribution to economic advancement.

THE ROAD TO INDUSTRIALIZATION

The biggest requirement for economic progress is, however, one that the churches are ill-equipped to meet. This is the need for massive capital that can be used to build up large-scale industry. There seem to be very few groups in the new nations who are in a position to supply this requirement and therein lies one of the greatest problems of these lands. Since private capital is so lacking, the new nations often must look to government to advance industrialization. This is the reason for the frequently expressed leaning toward some kind of "socialism" in the lands of Asia and Africa. It is not purely a theoretical preference for public as against private channels of development but a need to tap whatever resources for development are available. Combined with this is the desire to see the economic development guided by an over-all national purpose and a concern for the welfare of the whole population.

There is usually much place in this economy for industrialization under private auspices alongside the industrialization carried on by government, and this place may expand or contract depending on the resources available. There is also a crucial role in it for foreign capital, either private or governmental. The amount of foreign aid may not be large, but it can make a decisive difference in getting the economy moving. The "take-off point" for the economy, as it has been described by W. W. Rostow, is that point at which the economy develops a sufficient degree of momentum to enable it to move ahead to rapid industrialization under its own power. A certain rate of investment must be maintained by the economy, just as a certain rate of speed must be maintained by an airplane, if this take-off point is to be reached. Precise figures for the rate can be deceptive, but Barbara Ward suggests that somewhere between a 12 and a 15 per cent rate of investment is necessary to build up the capital resources to the take-off point. India, which provides the most outstanding example in these matters, has been able through its own efforts to raise its traditional 4 or 5 per cent rate up to 10 per cent and foreign aid has lifted it to 13 per cent. At this point the foreign aid may make the crucial difference in enabling the economy to move ahead vigorously rather than to languish in spotty development.

Christians who live in the older nations are thus put in the most strategic position to help with the crucial economic needs of the new lands. The support that they give to their governments and their industrialists in programs for technical assistance and export of capital to the new nations may be the most important help that they can provide for those countries. Their own societies accumulate capital easily and are even in danger of saving too much for their good. Therefore, both groups stand to gain when industries branch out with developments in the new nations. The governments of the industrialized lands also ought to make money available in loans without interest or even outright grants to the nations where capital is in such short supply.

The United States opened up a new era in the provision of international assistance with its Point Four Program adopted in 1949. But this has been far from adequate in terms of the needs. The total foreign aid received by most underdeveloped countries in the years since then has equaled on the average about one per cent of their national income. The aid, which has been given, has also been heavily concentrated in certain countries of military importance. Laos has received grants equaling as much as 20 per cent of its national income. In 1956-57, the twenty countries of the world with a per capita income under one hundred dollars received together just over a billion dollars in aid, but one-third of this went to South Korea and one-fourth to South Viet Nam, leaving less than half for the other eighteen. Short-term grants and the necessity for annual appropriations have also reduced the effectiveness of what by its nature is a long-term program. Steady development can be frustrated by unpredictable changes in aid.

The improvement of foreign aid programs from the West must be matched by the fullest use of the resources of the new nations themselves. They need to build up their exports so that they may gain capital through trade as well as aid. They are also in a position to help one another through economic assistance programs. Technical services provided by a slightly more advanced country are often more useful than the techniques that come from a very advanced land. Western technology has, because of the high cost of labor, often become so complicated that it is burdensome rather than helpful to a simple level of industry. As in the ecumenical mission of the church, so in international economic aid there should be no purely "sending" or "receiving" countries. All have something to gain from those that in some respects are more developed, and all have something to give to those that in some respects are less developed.

John Kenneth Galbraith, the Harvard economist who served as American ambassador in India, has called economic development for the new nations "the most important and humane task on which men are now engaged." [10] Christians of all nations are challenged to join hands in this most important task for the world. The service of the new church to the new nation here merges into the service of the world church to all nations. All should be involved. Not only the churches in their organized capacity are called on here but also all Christians in their various walks of life—the mechanics and engineers who can provide technical knowledge, the businessmen and bankers who can provide new industries and capital, the politicians and voters who can establish government aid programs. Whether they live in the new nations or the old, they are called on to help in the progress of those lands whose underdevelopment poses such a threat to the world.

[10] Galbraith, John Kenneth. *Economic Development in Perspective,* p. vi. Cambridge: Harvard University Press, 1962.

8

BEYOND THE NATION

WHEN Peter came to Antioch, he had to face a stern
rebuke. Paul had heard of his strange behavior
regarding table fellowship with Christians of other nations.
For a time, he had been willing to eat with them. But
then came men from the more conservative branch of the
church, and in their presence he was afraid. He separated
himself and refused to sit at table with those who were
not Jews. Paul "opposed him to his face, because he stood
condemned." (Galatians 2:11)

There were a number of issues in the argument. Peter's
behavior suggested that obedience to the Jewish law might
be necessary for a man's ultimate justification, and this
was what disturbed Paul most deeply. Dietary restrictions
based on religious regulations entered the picture. But tied
to these was the issue of full fellowship between Christians
of different national and cultural groups. Peter had not
actually demanded that the other nations follow the Jewish
law in addition to believing in Christ. He had agreed that

Paul should go to men of other nations. But when those men had come into the church he had withdrawn from full fellowship with them. For this "he stood condemned."

So must any church stand condemned that limits its fellowship and service to its own nation. This is true whether that nation be conceived in the biblical sense of one's own cultural group or in the modern sense of one's own nation-state. The church of Christ is for all men. It is not to be limited by national boundaries. Certainly the church within any nation must see itself as existing for the people of that nation. But it is not merely an organ of the national life. The confines of the nation do not set walls around its fellowship or service. It is still part of a worldwide body entrusted with a gospel for all mankind.

The churches in the new nations are in a better position than others to appreciate this fact of their existence. They do exist, very literally, as a result of the world embracing concern of Christians in other nations in very recent generations. If the limits of a church's responsibility were marked by national boundaries, there would be no churches in the new nations—or for that matter in most of the old nations, if we take a long enough view. We have seen how strong is the recognition among the churches of Asia and Africa of a call to help their nations in their difficulties. But that recognition is only part of what is happening; a more distant call is also being heard.

ALL ONE IN CHRIST JESUS

It is a peculiar thing, yet true, that as the churches of Asia and Africa have grown in a sense of responsibility for their own nations they have simultaneously grown in a sense of responsibility for the people of other nations. They have grown also in their fellowship with Christians of other nations. It seems that the increasing maturity that comes with selfhood in the church and nationhood in the land produces a readiness to take on a wider range of concerns and relationships.

We could have seen this growth very concretely if we had watched the movements of one stocky, brown-skinned man in the years when the new nations of Asia were first emerging. He could have been seen at almost any time of year traveling incessantly from India to Indonesia, and on to the Philippines, to Japan and Korea, and back again. His name was Rajah B. Manikam, and though he claimed India as his country of origin he made the whole of East Asia his homeland by his constant travels and his continuous contacts with its peoples. Working under the auspices of the World Council of Churches and the International Missionary Council, he tried to build up friendship and understanding among the churches scattered across the length of East Asia.

Rajah Manikam began his work with a conference of Asian churches held in Bangkok in 1949. This was the year that Indonesia gained its independence, the year after Ceylon and Burma and two years after India and Pakistan did the same. The Christians coming together on that occasion met with the joy of new discovery. In their separate colonial dependencies they had been only vaguely aware of one another. Now they found one another as neighbors and fellow workers in Christ. In the years that followed, as further meetings were held and Manikam carried forward his travels, the ties among them were drawn closer. Conferences were held on social problems, on theological education, and on missionary responsibilities.

Finally, in 1957, it was clear to them that they should form a continuing organization, which would bind them together in growing common concerns. At a meeting held in Sumatra that year, it was decided to establish a continuing East Asia Christian Conference, and two years later in Malaya the organization held its inaugural assembly. Now other men, such as Kyaw Than of Burma and D. T. Niles of Ceylon, followed in Manikam's footsteps and developed the common life further.

This same story can be repeated for Africa. Again, it was just at the time that African nations were blossoming into independence that the Christians of the continent discovered one another and came together for their first conference, this one held in Ibadan, Nigeria, in 1958. There, too, a continuing organization was founded, the All-Africa Conference of Churches, which convened its first assembly at Kampala, Uganda, in 1963. Donald M'Timkulu served as the African counterpart of Rajah Manikam, traveling up and down the continent building international contacts and awareness among Christians. He was followed as secretary in 1963 by Samuel H. Amissah of Ghana.

"NO EAST OR WEST"

The proffered hand of fellowship is not limited to Asian and African Churches. "Color bloc" isolationism, whatever appeal it may have for some people on those continents, is not acceptable to the Christians. When a conference of East Asian churches was held at Prapat in Indonesia shortly after the famous Bandung Conference of African and Asian States, the Prime Minister of Indonesia referred to the Christian gathering as a part of the fulfillment of Bandung. But the Christians at once pointed out that they harbored no desire to set up a color bloc in the church or become a separate body in the world Christian fellowship. The Bangkok Conference of 1949 was aware of the dangers of national interests. Its secretary said, "We must resist this temptation and fight it tooth and nail." This conference "is rightly of East Asia and for East Asia," he declared, "but it is at the same time of the ecumenical church and for the ecumenical church."

Most of the major Asian and African churches have exhibited a lively interest in the possibility of joining the world organizations of Christianity, particularly the World Council of Churches. As soon as the World Council was formed in 1948, the churches of Asia started to join it and *pari passu* with the coming of independence to Africa, the African churches began to take up membership. These churches have been among the most enthusiastic participants in the council, entering into all its departments and programs, contributing leadership to its staff, and challenging its conscience with new tasks and relationships. Those churches that have shown some reluctance in relation to the world bodies have done so for reasons of a theological or confessional nature rather than because of any limitation of their interests to their own nation.

HELPING HANDS ACROSS THE BORDER

Not only the desire for international fellowship but the desire to offer international service has entered the hearts of Christians in the new nations. The service that they are giving to their own nations seems to have encouraged a spirit of service to the people of other countries. Before the coming of national independence, there were scarcely any churches of Asia or Africa that thought of sending help to people in other lands. The only country from which a considerable Christian outreach was carried on was Japan, and Japan was, of course, the principal representative of an independent Asia. But with the new sense of national dignity and competence that has come in the wake of freedom, the churches of these lands have begun to feel that they, too, can and should send out evangelists, teachers, doctors, and nurses to help other nations. The arrangement of international assistance of this kind has been one of the prime functions of the East Asia Christian Conference. According to its reports more than two hundred missionaries from Asian churches are now serving across national boundaries. The churches of the Philippines have been the most outstanding in the number of their members whom they have sent to work in Indonesia, Thailand, Okinawa, Korea, the United States, and Iran. One denomination alone, the United Church of Christ in the Philippines, has nearly thirty missionaries at home and abroad. The churches in general have welcomed enthusiastically the idea of receiving help from other Asian or African Christians. Help from the churches of these continents is not subject to the suspicion of imperialism, which very naturally attaches to the activities of churches from the former imperialist powers.

But welcome assistance is not limited to that which comes from other new nations. The churches have also continued to call for helpers from the West. They have not declared, as they well might have in the heat of nationalist fervor and the pressure of nationalist demands, that Western workers were unwelcome. This was done by the churches in China after Communist rule was established and by the churches of Japan when the militarist control was at its height. But with an occasional small exception this is not the attitude that has been taken by the churches in the newly independent nations. There was a period of somewhat more than a year following Indonesia's independence when the churches of Java opposed the admission of foreign missionaries, but the opposition soon gave way to a warm welcome. Naturally the churches do not want missionaries from abroad who act in a way reminiscent of the old imperialism, but men and women who will share the vision and the struggle and the hard work that lie before the new nations are eagerly desired.

Such openness to contacts and receptiveness to assistance on the part of Christians in the new nations stands as a challenge to Christians of the older nations. If, in the midst of triumphant national sentiment, the Asians and Africans are eager to meet and talk with representatives from the Western churches, then the Westerners should be equally ready to meet them, to endeavor to understand them, and to interpret their national situation to the people of Europe and America. If, at a time of great national pressures, the Asians and Africans find it necessary to turn to the Western churches for help in nation-building and church-building, then the churches of the West should be equally ready to send aid through their purses and persons.

There is only one limitation that must be placed on the help that is sent from the West. The identification of the church with the people of the new nations must not be hidden or hindered by the help that comes from abroad. We have seen how important a change has been coming over the churches of the newly formed nations in recent years as they have grown in their sense of identification with and responsibility for the people among whom they live. This growth is to be fostered, and no aid should come in such a way or in such a quantity as to retard it. Sometimes the quantity has to be large. In Africa, for example, if the new nations are to meet the educational goals they have set, 60 per cent of their high school and college teachers will have to come from abroad. But in such cases it must be clearly recognized, as it normally is today, that the service given to the nation is the responsibility of the church in that nation and the work provided by Christians from other lands comes as an auxiliary effort to that of nationals.

"PUBLISH GLAD TIDINGS"

There is one kind of service given by the national church, often with assistance from abroad, which will stand as clear evidence of identification with the nation and yet will serve also as proof that the church is not just playing the role assigned to it by the nation. The service, which has this double function, is evangelism. In the work of evangelization, when it is rightly conceived and carried out, the national and the more-than-national are both evident.

The church, for its part, sees evangelism as the most

basic service that it can give to the nation because out of it grow all other forms of service. As Christians grow in a sense of identification with all the people of their nation, they wish to share with them that which means most in their own lives. Thus evangelistic work can, in a way, serve as a sign that the church is fully a part of the nation and is ready to serve the nation. We saw in an earlier chapter how the first flush of national feeling in the colonial lands produced certain outbursts of evangelistic activity. This early enthusiasm has, to some extent, continued into the period after independence. When, in 1955, the Christian youth in Djakarta staged a music festival presenting some of the great Christian music of the ages, they felt impelled to invite the wife of the President (her husband being out of the country at the time) and other high Muslim officials, who accepted their invitation. They would not, as they themselves admitted, have dreamed of doing such a thing before independence. It was because they had made common cause with their fellow countrymen, had suffered with them, and shared their common struggles that they were ready to open their hearts to them. Their evangelism showed their identification with the nation.

But the new nation, for its part, is rarely willing to accept evangelism as a desirable form of service, and this is where the more-than-national quality emerges. When the churches of the new nations carry on evangelism, they show that while they are dedicated to the service of the nation, they are not dedicated to serving the nation only as the nation wants to be served. Repeatedly, the newly triumphant nationalism has set its face against Christian evangelism. The national government of the Sudan in an attempt at the "Sudanization" of its southern provinces has enacted a series of stringent restrictions on missions, which have as a primary effect the reduction of evangelism among the southern peoples. Following the Sudanese Missionary Society Act of 1962, nearly all missionaries were expelled from the country. The use that has been made of the Ministry of Religious Affairs in Burma to propagate Buddhist preaching among the Karens even though a large proportion of Karens are Christians or animists is another example of national counteraction of Christian evangelism. Dr. Malalasekera, the nationalist Buddhist leader of Ceylon, has declared that conversion to Christianity "has all manner of undesirable associations" including "corruption and denationalization." Paul Devanandan in his book, *The Gospel and Renascent Hinduism,* has told how Hindu nationalists are urging a reinterpretation of Christianity that would weaken evangelism. They look upon evangelism as a threat to national unity and to the tolerance that should exist between people of the same nation. As Devanandan suggests, this shows the need for a careful rethinking by both Hindus and Christians as to what they mean by evangelism. Christian evangelism, when rightly conceived and practiced, is not opposed to national unity nor to tolerance. As for unity, evangelism is an expression of love on the part of one religious community for the other people of the nation, thus expressing a much deeper and stronger form of unity than could come from a simple glossing over of religious differences. As regards tolerance, evangelism carries with it a recognition of the freedom and integrity of the person evangelized, thus expressing a deeper and stronger tolerance than comes from mere indifference to other peoples' beliefs.

Despite the problems raised by the nation, in place after place evangelism goes on. We can see it in East Java, where the Javanese Christians have opened up a new mission to villagers and begun some new village churches. Or, again, it appears on a small island in the Philippines where the six churches of a decade ago have produced six more through their active Sunday school program. In Burma, the various Baptist Conventions maintain a whole line of mission stations of their own among the hill peoples. In Tanganyika, the Sonjo Mission of the Lutheran Church of Northern Tanganyika has begun to produce a new church among the Sonjo people. In Ghana, the Christians of the South are awakening to a new concern for evangelism among the people of the North. The most important thing about these efforts is that in all of them the national churches themselves are taking responsibility. A generation ago those nationals who engaged in evangelism did so under the direction and as the employees of the foreign missionaries. In much of Africa this is still the case. But in Asia where the sense of national identity had an earlier start and where the coming patterns for Africa can therefore be discerned, the initiative and direction for evangelism have normally passed into the hands of the nationals, and the foreign missionaries work as their helpers. Under the new arrangement, it often happens that there is less actual evangelistic work done—though Korea is a notable exception in this respect—but the work that is done has a great significance for the future because it expresses the dedication of the people themselves.

FOR THE NATION AND THE KINGDOM

The work of evangelism stands then as a clear indication that the church can become national without being at the same time "nationalized." It provides a kind of roadsign pointing the way out of the contemporary perplexities surrounding the place of the nation. Can the universal Kingdom be served in the serving of the nation? Yes, but the service will not always be what the nation expects. It will be the better service for that reason, however. In new nations as in old, in the East as in the West, the serving of the Kingdom of God will prove to be the surest way of building up the nation on firm foundations. Those citizens will serve the nation most truly who see their service within the context of the demands of truth and justice, who seek to advance the welfare of their own people in keeping with the welfare of other peoples. The church will be able to render better service to the nation just because of the fact that it acknowledges a higher loyalty and a wider concern than the nation itself. In the words of the Thessalonica Conference:

The church's struggle for the freedom to worship and witness to Christ as Lord of the nation, to keep its fellowship open to all men irrespective of colour or other communal affiiliation, and to have relations with churches outside the nation, is at the same time its contribution to the development of a healthy nationalism.[1]

[1] World Council of Churches, International Ecumenical Study Conference, Thessalonica, Greece, 1959. *Dilemmas and Opportunities, Christian Action in Rapid Social Change.* Geneva: World Council of Churches, 1959.

The nation is not truly served by those citizens who are dominated by a narrow nationalism. That form of fanaticism has too often driven peoples along the path that leads to their own destruction. Nor is it most truly served by those who make a religion of their patriotism—the desperate ones who would be utterly lost if they did not have their national pride to cling to. In times of great pressure, such as the new nations are facing, the demand may be heard for men of this type. But the nation should know that actually it will receive more useful, thoughtful, well-balanced service from those whose devotion does not spring from such desperation, but from an unfaltering trust in God, in whom they find a rock of assurance, come what may in national affairs, and by whom they are called into the love and service of their fellow-countrymen.

The days that lie ahead will not be easy ones for the churches. The mountainous problems their homelands face indicate a time of sacrifice and testing to come. In this the churches will need understanding and support from Christians of the West. They will need, even more, a sustaining vision of their own as to the place that their nation occupies in the purpose of God and the way in which their service will contribute to that purpose. Inspired by such a vision, their prayer can well be that they may

> In ire and exultation
> Aflame with faith, and free,
> Lift up a living nation,
> A single sword to Thee.[1]

[1] Chesterton, G. K. (1874-1936), Hymn No. 562, *The English Hymnal*. London: Oxford University Press, 1945.

SUGGESTIONS FOR
FURTHER READING

Abrecht, Paul. *The Churches and Rapid Social Change.* New York: Doubleday and Co., Inc., 1961. The most complete and interesting account of what the churches have thought and done about the great changes that are taking place in Asia and Africa, of which the establishment of new nations is one.

Baron, S. W. *Modern Nationalism and Religion.* New York: Harper and Brothers, 1947. A thorough study of the varied experiences that Catholics, Protestants, Orthodox, and Jews have had with nationalism in recent centuries.

Benham, Frederic Charles. *Economic Aid to Underdeveloped Countries.* New York: Oxford University Press, 1961. A well written, brief account that avoids no issues. Covers private investment and trade as well as governmental aid to the new nations.

Daniels, George M. *This Is the Church in New Nations.* New York: Friendship Press, 1964. A concise treatment of the problems faced by the church in newly independent nations, illustrated with photographs.

Devanandan, P. D., and Thomas, M. M. *Christian Participation in Nation Building.* Bangalore: National Christian Council of India, 1960. The fullest report from any of the new nations on the way in which Christians are thinking about their life in and responsibilities to the nation.

Emerson, Rupert. *From Empire to Nation: The Rise to Self-Assertion of the Asian and African Peoples.* Cambridge: Harvard University Press, 1960. A splendid general coverage of all that is involved in the appearance of new nations.

Galbraith, John Kenneth. *Economic Development in Perspective.* Cambridge: Harvard University Press, 1962. A short and interesting exposition of the kind of problems that are faced by the underdeveloped countries. By one of America's most widely read economists.

Morris, Colin. *The Hour After Midnight.* New York: Longmans, Green and Co., Inc., 1961. A lively personal history of a pastor's involvement in the struggle for the birth of a new nation in Africa.

Sayre, Leslie. *This Rocket Called Freedom.* New York: Friendship Press, 1964. A novel centering around three African students and an American nurse who has gone to Africa as a fraternal worker for a mission board.

Smith, Wilfred Cantwell. *Islam in Modern History.* Princeton: Princeton University Press, 1957. A perceptive and sympathetic analysis of what has been happening as nationalism and other forces grip the world of Islam. Also available in paperback form.

Taylor, John V. *Christians of the Copperbelt.* London: SCM Press, 1961. An on-the-spot study of the life of Christians in the midst of new nationalism and industrialization.

Ward, Barbara. *The Rich Nations and the Poor Nations.* New York: W. W. Norton and Co., Inc., 1962. A brief and lucid statement of a great problem that faces the world and what needs to be done about it.

ABOUT THE FORMAT

Type: *Linotype Fairfield 11 point leaded 2 points*

Composition, press, and binding: *The Colonial Press, Inc., Clinton, Massachusetts*

Covers: *Affiliated Lithographers, Inc., New York*

Text paper: *S. D. Warren's Number 66 Antique*

Typographic design: *Margery W. Smith*